The
Writer's
Style

The Writer's Style

A Rhetorical Field Guide

Paul Butler

UTAH STATE UNIVERSITY PRESS

Logan

© 2018 by University Press of Colorado

Published by Utah State University Press
An imprint of University Press of Colorado
245 Century Circle, Suite 202
Louisville, Colorado 80027

 The University Press of Colorado is a proud member of the Association of University Presses.

The University Press of Colorado is a cooperative publishing enterprise supported, in part, by Adams State University, Colorado State University, Fort Lewis College, Metropolitan State University of Denver, Regis University, University of Colorado, University of Northern Colorado, Utah State University, and Western State Colorado University.

∞ This paper meets the requirements of the ANSI/NISO Z39.48–1992 (Permanence of Paper).

ISBN: 978-1-60732-809-4 (pbk.)
ISBN: 978-1-60732-810-0 (ebook)
DOI: https://doi.org/10.7330/9781607328100

Library of Congress Cataloging-in-Publication Data

Names: Butler, Paul, date. author.
Title: The writer's style : a rhetorical field guide / Paul Butler.
Description: Logan : Utah State University Press, [2018] | Includes bibliographical references and index.
Identifiers: LCCN 2018004886| ISBN 9781607328094 (pbk. : alk. paper) | ISBN 9781607328100 (ebook)
Subjects: LCSH: Language and languages—Style—Study and teaching (Higher) | Rhetoric—Study and teaching (Higher)
Classification: LCC P53.27 .W74 2018 | DDC 808/.042—dc23
LC record available at https://lccn.loc.gov/2018004886

Contents

Figures

Acknowledgments

A map says to you, "Read me carefully, follow me closely, doubt me not." It says, "I am the earth in the palm of your hand. Without me, you are alone and lost."

And indeed you are. Were all the maps in this world destroyed and vanished under the direction of some malevolent hand, each man would be blind again, each city be made a stranger to the next, each landmark become a meaningless signpost pointing to nothing.

Yet, looking at it, feeling it, running a finger along its lines, it is a cold thing, a map, humourless and dull, born of calipers and a draughtsman's board. That coastline there, that ragged scrawl of scarlet ink, shows neither sand nor sea nor rock; it speaks of no mariner, blundering full sail in wakeless seas, to bequeath, on sheepskin or a slab of wood, a priceless scribble to posterity. This brown blot that marks a mountain has, for the casual eye, no other significance, though twenty men, or ten, or only one, may have squandered life to climb it. Here is a valley, there a swamp, and there a desert; and here is a river that some curious and courageous soul, like a pencil in the hand of God, first traced with bleeding feet.

—BERYL MARKHAM, WEST WITH THE NIGHT

I begin with Beryl Markham in part because her writing represents an example of the kind of stylistic genius demonstrated by authors featured in *The Writer's Style*. I am grateful every day for writers like Markham—writers whose work graces the pages of this book—who inspire me, move me, compel me to pick up pen, pencil, or laptop to write another day. Markham's excerpt also suggests the subtitle, *A Rhetorical Field Guide*, and the way the text is a mapping of style meant to probe language from various angles: to trace, uncover, and analyze the rhetorical effects of words, sentences, paragraphs, images, and the meanings underlying them.

All maps are rhetorical, intended to guide readers with an argument, a message. My map of *The Writer's Style* begins in Los Angeles, where Frederic Speers approached me after my RSA-affiliated MLA panel and invited me to write a book that has since evolved significantly. I am indebted to Fred for his ideas, insights, and enthusiasm. I am also obliged to my aunt, Sally Butler, and niece, Aislinn Hettermann, who offered encouragement and support for the project as we laughed and talked together at Sally's home during a break from the MLA conference.

In writing the book, I benefited greatly from the detailed feedback of twenty-three anonymous reviewers, whose candid responses improved the book incalculably and whose advice has formed a significant part of the "key" to this field guide's map. Of that venerable group, one reader, T. R. Johnson of Tulane University, allowed one of his quotes to be featured publicly on the cover of *The Writer's Style*, a generous offer for which I am extremely thankful.

Furthermore, I can never recognize adequately the contributions of two colleagues: Jim Zebroski, who read every word of the book on several occasions and offered enormously useful commentary, always in highly generative ways, and Star Medzerian Vanguri, who provided analysis and advice with unparalleled insight along with practical readings of the book, its effects, and its pedagogical implications, all rendered with unfailing patience and good will. Stated simply, without Jim and Star, *The Writer's Style* would not be the book it has become.

I am grateful to colleagues at the University of Houston whose help was immensely important at various stages of the project: Nathan Shepley, who wrote with me at Black Hole, EQ Heights, and Catalina Coffee, where we also engaged in lively conversations about writing; Lorraine Stock and Margot Backus, who read the book at a near-final stage and offered exceptionally smart advice; and J. Kastely, who gave prescient feedback on the book at a critical point and provided unremitting encouragement. I also thank all of my other colleagues within or closely affiliated with the Department of English for their friendship and support. My gratitude extends to the many students, graduate and undergraduate, who have offered their honest feedback and gracious commentary.

Also invaluable to me at the University of Houston was the Martha Gano Houstoun Endowment, in the Department of English, which allowed me to work with colleagues to test and complicate my ideas as part of the Digital Media and Composition Institute at The Ohio State University and the Digital Humanities Summer Institute at the University of Victoria. I am also fortunate to have benefited from a Project Completion Grant awarded by the UH College of Liberal Arts and Social Sciences, which helped the book reach its final stages, and the Provost's Travel Fund, which allowed me to discuss my ideas on style at renowned national conferences. My appreciation also goes to the UH Copyright Team.

The book would not be possible without the vision, guidance, and advice of Michael Spooner, the former acquisitions editor at Utah State University Press, whose generosity is equaled only by his acumen; Michael is missed by countless colleagues in Rhetoric and Composition, and yet, in a final selfless act, Michael chose a brilliant successor in Rachael Levay, who has graciously offered sage advice and has worked tirelessly to improve the book. Kylie Haggen, Utah State University Press's assistant editor extraordinaire, has assisted superbly with many technical aspects of the publishing process. It has also been a privilege to work with the team at the University Press of Colorado: Beth Svinarich, sales and marketing manager, whose copy writing is inspired; Dan Pratt, production manager, who designed the cover and interior pages to great acclamation; Laura Furney, assistant director and managing editor, who oversaw the whole process patiently and professionally; Kami Day, copyeditor, whose rhetorical expertise provided invaluable guidance; and Darrin Pratt, director, whose leadership expertly guides a vital scholarly enterprise.

Beyond these collective groups, I am beholden to my style family, individuals whose work has motivated me and whose collaboration has been enormously satisfying in ways too numerous to mention. To that end, I thank, first, Frank Farmer, a remarkable mentor and friend, whose work and philosophy always surprise me; Brian Ray, who has been a fine and trusted colleague; Louise Weatherbee Phelps, whose faithful counsel has made my current work possible; and Nora Bacon, Bill FitzGerald, Melissa Goldwaithe, Becky Howard, T. R. Johnson, Andrea Olinger, Tom Pace, Mike Duncan, Zak Lancaster, Jarron Slater, and Star Vanguri. I am also excited to welcome new voices to the fold, namely, Cyndey Alexis, Laura Aull, Anthony Box, Jimmy Butts, Lynee Gaillet, Eric House, Almas Khan, Eric Leake, Rich Rice, and Jon Udelson.

I also want to acknowledge family members Tod and Katie Butler, who provide unshakable anchorage for my efforts, along with Josh, Koda, and Austin Butler and Amber Krieger; Aislinn, Matt, Dylan, and Blake Hettermann; and Jaida, Chris, Pacey, Brighton, and Archer Harris.

As the lengthy route of this book reaches its destination, my compass now points in different directions, a sign of new things to come. My brief section thus ends where it began, with Beryl Markham, who says that a mariner—or, by extension, a draftsman, or a writer—hopes his map, or her work, will "bequeath, on sheepskin or a slab of wood, a priceless scribble to posterity."

Preface

The Writer's Style (*TWS*) is informed by centuries of stylistic and rhetorical theory and history. The book draws upon many of the debates that have shaped the study of style over the years, and it takes seriously the important scholarship that has made up the field of stylistic study, including recent work within the field of rhetoric and composition. Thus, *TWS* is written with a deep knowledge base and an understanding of the different approaches and directions the study of style has taken in its long history.

While *The Writer's Style* cites, sometimes explicitly, some of the research important to stylistic study, the book is not a historical account of style. Instead, *TWS* is designed to help *guide* writers who wish to incorporate style in their writing. It provides a synthesis of stylistic concepts and practices. It analyzes *how* writers use style and examines the *effects* of their stylistic and rhetorical decisions on meaning. It is a *rhetorical* guide in that it considers the writer's purpose, the context or occasion in which they are writing, and their audience. (*The Writer's Style* uses singular *they* in the interest of gender inclusion.)

In analyzing the effects of a writer's choices, *The Writer's Style* cannot know whether someone's stylistic decisions are conscious or unconscious. In fact, it is often hard, even for experienced writers, to state, after the fact, why they made certain choices. Nonetheless, the book approaches stylistic choices as *deliberate* ones and offers many resources to help writers use style *deliberately* in their writing, either by making conscious choices about style or by internalizing, and then incorporating, *TWS*'s stylistic resources. These resources are intended to help writers understand the consequences of their choices and to use style to create and communicate meaning effectively.

■ ORGANIZATION OF CHAPTERS

The Writer's Style combines inductive and deductive approaches in analyzing, evaluating, and discussing style. Induction begins with specific instances or examples and moves toward broader generalizations or theories, while deduction moves from general to specific, from premises to logical conclusion(s). In that vein, chapters generally follow a recognizable organizational structure, sometimes repeated within individual chapters:

- *Introduction of Exemplary Text(s)*: Chapters often begin with a specific exemplary text or texts, presented or "performed" by their authors, the examples part of an *inductive* approach.
- *Analysis*: The next move is to an analysis of the exemplary text or texts, drawing conclusions or inferences based on one or more features of the text(s). This analysis is *deductive*.
- *Application(s)*: Chapters continue with one or more applications that deepen or complicate the concept or stylistic resource just analyzed, often combining *inductive* and *deductive* approaches.

■ STYLE AS LINGUA FRANCA

One goal of the book is to make style a kind of lingua franca, or common language, as William FitzGerald (2013) has suggested, by drawing frequently upon and deploying a wide array of resources. For that reason, stylistic concepts introduced in one chapter are likely to reappear—in different contexts, with varying effects—in one or more subsequent chapters. Thus, the very act of reading *TWS* will reinforce ideas in useful ways. Here are some specific ways that happens—and some of the benefits that emerge from style as lingua franca.

■ Analysis, Interpretation, and Imitation

TWS assumes that an emphasis on stylistic *analysis* is a crucial part of interpretation, or the "interpretive act" (Kent 1999). The interpretive act is meant in the postprocess sense that interpretation belongs not only to the reception but the production of discourse. In other words, *TWS* assumes writers will learn from, and internalize, the book's extensive stylistic analysis to help them produce effective prose. Winston Churchill (1930, 16) adopted a similar strategy, saying he "continually [practiced] English analysis" to learn "the essential structure of the ordinary British sentence." In that regard, analysis is a form of *imitation*, which, says James J. Murphy (1987, xxx), employs "models to learn how others have used language." *TWS* also treats imitation as verbatim copying, paraphrase, and transforming a writer's words and subject matter.

■ Argument

An additional benefit of style as lingua franca is to find different ways to make arguments with stylistic devices. One such device is the *figure of speech*, "a form of speech artfully varied from common usage" in the words of Roman orator Quintilian (Murphy 1987, 67). *TWS* divides figures of speech into *schemes*, deviations in the normal order or arrangement of words (e.g., alliteration or climax), and *tropes*, which Richard Lanham (1991) calls "turns" in the meaning of a word (e.g., paradox or metaphor).

How are figures of speech a part of argument? Quintilian (1921, 359) emphasized the utility of the figures of speech, saying that while it may *seem* that "proof is infinitesimally affected by the figures employed," in reality the figures "lend credibility to our arguments"; constitute an "effective method of exciting the emotions"; and "win approval for our characters as pleaders," thus tying the schemes and tropes to the argumentative appeals of *logos*, *pathos*, and *ethos*. Rhetorician Kenneth Burke, says Jeanne Fahnestock (1999, 35), recognized "the ability of figures to express a certain line of argument and simultaneously to induce an audience to participate in that argument." *TWS* helps writers make arguments by integrating schemes and tropes in their prose.

Other aspects of style are also closely related to argument. For example, the emphasis on clarity, concision, cohesion, and emphasis in this book offers ways for writers and speakers to make arguments persuasively. The use of varying sentence structure also contributes to the effects arguments have on intended audiences.

■ HEURISTICS

Most chapters also include *heuristics*, or aids to understanding and discovery, that allow writers to think more about the concepts that have been introduced. Sometimes it is useful to consider another example to think through problems with style in a new context, with varied audiences, or on a different level. With the book's multiple audiences and varied objectives in mind, the following heuristics are interspersed in *TWS*:

- *Take Two*: These brief interludes take up recently introduced concepts from a slightly different angle, offering a fresh perspective or a new way of looking at some aspect of style.

- *Do-It-Yourself (DIY)*: This heuristic offers readers and writers the chance to think in depth about concepts that have been introduced and to apply the knowledge they have gained to slightly different contexts or audiences. It goes along with the book's inherently rhetorical approach and offers writers a chance to test their understanding of new concepts.

- *Critical Thinking*: Questions in the "Critical Thinking" sections at the end of most chapters invite readers to extend their thinking and to reflect upon the rich applications of the stylistic knowledge imparted in the chapter.

- *Chapter 11 Practice*: Readers and writers can turn regularly to chapter 11 for a series of productive assignments and ideas for practicing style.

◼ TEXTUAL, VISUAL, AND DIGITAL EXCERPTS

The Writer's Style includes a number of diverse textual excerpts, including those drawn from digital, multimodal, visual, and social media sources, to help writers discover and develop their own style. Because of style's rich history, *TWS* casts a wide net in using sample texts, showing how important style is and has been throughout the years. The book also attempts to include authors who embody *diversity* in the many senses of that word. What's more, one of the book's main arguments is that style makes writing memorable, keeping some texts alive for decades, or centuries, and *The Writer's Style* makes that argument in part by drawing upon writing that continues to resonate with readers years after it first appeared.

The Writer's Style is not prescriptive, but *generative*. The text introduces readers and writers to an array of innovative stylistic resources. It offers unique ways to think about style and to develop knowledge of the stylistic techniques available in writing for different audiences, rhetorical situations, and practical, academic, or artistic purposes.

The
Writer's
Style

1   An Introduction to Style

When something we read, see, or hear affects us profoundly, how do we write or speak about it effectively? If we are inspired by a certain je ne sais quoi, an ineffable quality, say, in Vincent van Gogh's (1889) *Starry Night*, what lexical and rhetorical choices are available to us to describe the way we think or feel? Where do we find the appropriate words to fit the circumstances?

One answer to these questions is to say that everyone draws on a distinctive *way* of writing or speaking called *style*. Style can vary depending on the context, purpose, and audience, so we might have not only *a* style but a *range* of styles with common features. The same individual, for example, is likely to make different stylistic choices in an e-mail to a boss about an online safety campaign, an academic essay proposing a new definition of sustainability, a eulogy at a friend's funeral, or the introduction of an international speaker at a professional lecture.

Some think of style as a voice speaking, the idea that writing is an extension of talking. In that light, Otis Winchester (1972, x) says developing a style involves "learning the sound of your voice." He stresses the importance of sound and voice and advises writers to talk and listen to themselves; to listen to the talk of others; to read aloud from other writers' prose as well as "from your own prose—and listen for *your* voice," adding,

DOI: 10.7330/9781607328100.c001

Starry Night (La nuit etoilée) by Vincent van Gogh, painting, oil on canvas, Saint-Rémy, June 1889 (MOMA)

Speak freely through the page as if your hand on the pen or typewriter were an organ of speech—and write as if you were conversing face to face with your reader.

Winchester might have drawn his advice from Mark Twain, whose informal, or colloquial, speech "sounds in our ears with the immediacy of the heard voice," according to Lionel Trilling (1950, 17). Twain's style is often connected to his Southern heritage, reflected, for example, in the vernacular English of Huck Finn: "But I reckon I got to light out for the Territory ahead of the rest, because Aunt Sally she's going to adopt me and sivilize me and I can't stand it. I been there before" (Twain 1994, 220).

The proposition that everyone has a unique or distinctive style, tied in some respects to speech (or to a voice speaking), implies a connection to one's personality, a concept for which French encyclopedist George-Louis Leclerc, Compte de Buffon, coined the saying "style is the man." Buffon's adage suggests style is an inherent part of identity.

Take, for instance, Ernest Hemingway, described by the *New York Times* (1981) as "tight-lipped," with a "terse vocabulary" and "tough idiomatic voice," terms associated not only with his style but with his identity as a "macho icon" (Gopnik 2017). In her autobiography, *I Know Why the Caged Bird Sings*, Maya Angelou (1969) adopts a voice and style that weave together the slave narrative and church sermon, according to Harold Bloom (1996), both part of the African American oral tradition and of the author's group identity. That communal identity draws on the style of Southern speech patterns, with expressions like "didn't cotton to" or "he gonna be that kind of nasty" (Lupton 1998).

If we consider style as part of identity, is it accurate to say we are "born" with a style, with no power to control or change it? On the contrary, *The Writer's Style* argues, it is possible to study and analyze a writer's style and to learn how their stylistic choices have specific effects. These effects, whether based on a writer's conscious or unconscious decisions, can be used to influence, and possibly change, the way we think of ourselves as writers. By studying a person's style, we can discover stylistic features we might use deliberately to transform our own writing.

Style, then, gives us the ability to think critically about writing. Can studying style also help solve familiar writing problems? It can demonstrate how writers have dealt with writing issues in various contexts. Does it reveal the "rules" of academic discourse? Not explicitly, perhaps, but it does show the strategies writers have used to address academic and other audiences for different purposes. Everyone has a stake in learning about style. It can change how we think about writing, especially in a digital age.

To get an idea of style at work, consider UCLA professor and art historian Albert Boime's (1984, 93) response to van Gogh's masterpiece, *Starry Night*. Boime was interested in the "celestial phenomena" in van Gogh's work, comparing the painting itself with contemporaneous astronomical conditions during the artist's stay at the St. Rémy asylum. If it is true that style helps capture ineffable qualities in a work and reflects aspects of speech or the speaking voice, how can that be seen in Boime's piece? To answer that question, first consider the way Boime introduces van Gogh's painting:

> What is it that we see in the picture? There is first of all the sight of a night sky teeming with stellar life: the waning moon with its aureole, a network of white, yellow, orange, and blue stars which seem to rotate and pulsate and throw out cosmic energy, and a spiraling band turning on itself while running parallel to the horizon. Beneath this active sky we glimpse the houses of a hamlet surrounded by wheatfields and olive groves and bounded on the right by foothills whose undulations are repeated by light streaks in the sky.

■ STYLE IN BOIME'S DESCRIPTION OF VAN GOGH'S PAINTING

While the paragraph seems simply to describe the painting, Boime actually shows his affinity for van Gogh's work of art through *style*. How does he do so? His primary technique is to slow down his explanations, as though he is savoring all details of *Starry Night* and preserving them for readers. Hence, after asking—as one might in speaking—"What is it that we see in the picture?," he prepares readers for his answer with a syntactic device ("There is"), delaying his point by moving it to later in the sentence, followed by metadiscourse ("first of all"), a referential phrase that anticipates additional details.

Boime's question (indicative of conversation), syntax, and metadiscourse set up his use of what Francis Christensen (1963) calls a "cumulative sentence," which begins with a main or "base" clause ("There is first of all the sight of a night sky teeming with stellar life") and adds details in a series of free modifiers (e.g., "the waning moon with its aureole, a network of white, yellow, orange, and blue stars which seem to rotate and pulsate and throw out cosmic energy, and a spiraling band turning on itself while running parallel to the horizon"). The "free" modifiers, optional phrases that can be easily moved within the sentence (see chapter 7), suggest what Boime sees as crucial in the painting.

Boime's obvious admiration for *Starry Night* can also be seen in his use of a figure of speech, an artful variation from normal usage. Boime employs a *scheme*, or deviation in word arrangement, called *polysyndeton*, the deliberate and abundant use of conjunctions, as we see in these examples: "a network of white, yellow, orange, and blue stars which seem to rotate *and* pulsate *and* throw out cosmic energy"; "Beneath this active sky we glimpse the houses of a hamlet surrounded by wheatfields *and* olive groves *and* bounded on the right by foothills." Boime's use of "and" slows the pace of his description, as though he wishes to relish every detail, experience each discovery anew, and stress the painting's cumulative effect. Polysyndeton lets him achieve that result.

It is worth noting briefly that along with his use of polysyndeton, Boime also contrasts the active night sky in the painting with what he considers the artist's more subdued portrayal of the surrounding landscape. Stylistically, this change is reflected in his use of the passive voice: "Beneath this active sky we glimpse the house of a hamlet *surrounded by wheatfields* and olive groves and *bounded on the right by foothills*." Unlike the active verbs used, for example, to describe the stars ("rotate," "pulsate," "throw out"), the passive voice removes agency from van Gogh's portrayal of the house and the surrounding countryside, reflecting the contrast Boime sees in the painting itself.

The use of the passive voice also diverges from the way Boime animates celestial aspects of van Gogh's painting through a *trope*, a turn in meaning called *personification*, bestowing human qualities on inanimate objects: "a night sky *teeming with stellar life*"; an "*active* sky"; the foothills' "*undulations*"; and "a *spiraling band turning on itself* while *running parallel* to the horizon." He also calls attention to the painting's dynamic astronomical features by attributing human qualities to the church spire and cypress tree.

> In the center of the hamlet is a church with its *spire barely breaking the horizon line* while at the left a *cypress tree towers* over the entire composition, *propelling itself into the animated firmament*. (emphasis added)

Boime adds to the effect of personification with the scheme of *alliteration*, the repetition of similar consonant sounds, with "*b*arely *b*reaking" and "*t*ree *t*owers over the en*t*ire." The alliteration contrasts the opposing proportions of the ("barely breaking") spire and the towering tree, calling attention to the significance of their relative sizes, and the role they play, in van Gogh's "apocalyptic exaltation" in *Starry Night*.

■ STYLE IN BOIME'S ARTICLE TITLE

How is Boime's interest also apparent stylistically in the very title of his *Arts Magazine* article, "Van Gogh's *Starry Night*: A History of Matter and A Matter of History"? In his title, Boime uses more than one figure of speech, a scheme called *antimetabole*, words repeated in reverse grammatical order in successive phrases or clauses: "A History of Matter and a Matter of History." The unusual syntax gives his title an aphoristic quality, signaling his interest in both history and science in the work of art.

Adding to the effect of the repetition is Boime's use of a trope, *antanaclasis*, a type of pun, or play on words, in which the same word is repeated in two different senses. He uses "matter" first to denote the astronomical substance of the work and second to give its more common meaning of a subject. "History" first signifies a narrative of past events and then a branch of knowledge.

Why is it useful to analyze the style of the title? Through his focus on repetition, or reversal, involving deviation from normal word order and meaning, Boime encourages readers to recognize that understanding and interpreting van Gogh's painting requires a new approach. The figures of speech Boime uses are forms of *antithesis*, in which contrasting ideas are juxtaposed syntactically, accentuating the writer's focus on the oppositions in *Starry Night* and the turmoil of an artist "incarcerated in both mind and spirit"—one who depicts a cypress tree as "tree of death" and "symbol of immortality."

Overall, the writer's use of style helps bring van Gogh's canvas to life, conveying his veneration of the artist's work. Boime's stylistic decisions indicate not only his passion for van Gogh's rendering of "celestial phenomena" but also his analysis of the astronomical activity as reflecting upheavals in the artist's mind as well as more subdued aspects of the painting. Boime's style reveals his "take" on van Gogh's chef-d'oeuvre.

2 | What Is Style?

From time to time, often when we least expect it, words can make us stop and listen, capturing our attention for reasons we may not fully understand. What makes these words memorable? Why, for instance, can so many of us recite the opening of Abraham Lincoln's (1863) Gettysburg Address?

> Four score and seven years ago our fathers brought forth on this continent a new nation, conceived in liberty and dedicated to the proposition that all men are created equal.

Or recall what Neil Armstrong said as the first person to walk on the moon:

> That's one small step for a man, one giant leap for mankind.
> (Wilford 1969)

The Writer's Style argues that we remember these sentences because of their *style*.

■ STYLE AS A WAY OF WRITING

Style is a way of writing, the *manner* in which we use vocabulary, word choice, tone, voice, figures of speech (like parallelism or irony), and many other language features to achieve *effects*

DOI: 10.7330/9781607328100.c002

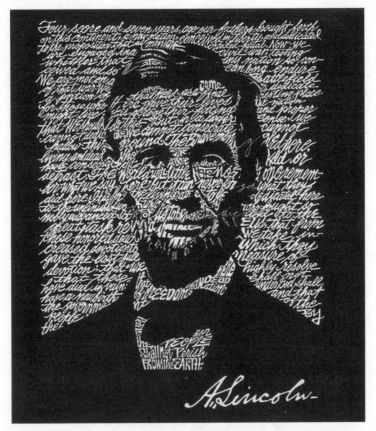

Abraham Lincoln and the Gettysburg Address

in writing or speaking. *How* something is said—its *style*—is intrinsically related to *what* is said—its *content*. The study of style asks, *how* are specific effects produced, either consciously or unconsciously, in our use of language?

To answer that question, consider the opening of the Gettysburg Address, in which several aspects contribute to Lincoln's style. First, he begins with unusual word choice, or *diction*: "Four score and seven years ago." He could have written "eighty-seven years ago," but his diction heightens the solemnity of dedicating a Civil War cemetery. What's more, the phrase has a rising and falling *rhythm*, a stylistic feature that creates expectations in readers, helping us anticipate what will follow.

Lincoln also makes an apparent reference, or *allusion*, to language in the Bible, in which a person's lifespan is said to be "threescore years and ten," a phrase from Psalms with which the president's audience would likely have been familiar. This biblical allusion suggests that style involves the use of language features within and *beyond* words and sentences. As Lincoln's allusion shows, style extends to paragraphs, to essays or entire books, and to elements outside the work itself.

As a way of writing, style depends on the interplay of not just one but many stylistic elements. John Middleton Murry (1922, 70) points out style's interactive nature: "Style is not an isolable quality of writing; it is writing itself." That is, style is essential to all aspects of language, to our own and others' writing. Its importance is apparent in how we express ourselves every time we write or speak. *TWS* assumes writers or speakers are using style consciously, or deliberately, but their use of style may, in fact, be unconscious; they may be unaware of the explicit stylistic resources they employ.

■ TAKE 2

The image of Lincoln that opens this chapter, with the text of the Gettysburg Address superimposed on the president's profile, recalls Buffon's saying from the introduction that "style is the man." The instance of visual rhetoric reflects the idea that it can be difficult to separate a person's identity from their style. Lincoln is remembered for the Gettysburg Address and other speeches he made as president. His style has many distinctive features we associate with his writing and speaking.

■ DO IT YOURSELF (DIY)

How is individual expression, or identity, closely tied to the sound of one's voice? Consider the way Dorothy Allison (1995) uses style to express her southern heritage:

> I was born trash in a land where the people all believe themselves natural aristocrats. Ask any white Southerner. They'll take you back to generations, say, "Yeah, we had a plantation." The hell we did.

Response to DIY prompt: Here is one possible response to the DIY heuristic to suggest how readers and writers might analyze the excerpt from Dorothy Allison:

> In this example, we can hear Allison's speaking voice when she writes "I was born trash" and "The hell we did." The clauses are examples of *colloquial*, or informal, conversational language and are part of her self-expression. The colloquialisms, along with her *tone*, that is, her attitude toward her readers and subject matter, convey her feeling of honesty for her roots and her reproval of those trying to put on airs about their past. They reflect her *Southern identity* through her conversational style and ironic tone, with her clause "The hell we did" indicating that the actual meaning of those who say "Yeah, we had a plantation" is just the opposite of what it seems to be.

■ STYLE AS CONTEXTUAL AND RHETORICAL

In achieving various effects, the words we choose, and the style we adopt, exist not in a void or vacuum but in a specific *context*—the *setting*, *situation*, or *occasion* in which we write or speak about a certain topic. The context of the Gettysburg Address, for example, was the dedication of Soldiers' National Cemetery during the Civil War. Lincoln's phrase "Four score and seven years ago" refers to the date of the Declaration of Independence.

Given the moon landing—the context of Neil Armstrong's sentence "That's one small step for a man, one giant leap for mankind"—the effect of the parallel contrast, or *antithesis*, between "one *small step* for a man" and "one *giant leap* for mankind" is to portray Armstrong's footstep as having far-reaching consequences: not only touching the moon's surface but also transcending it. By juxtaposing the two clauses, he propels the audience into a new era of human progress, his words moving from a literal meaning (a footstep) to a metaphorical, or implied, one (a leap in human advancement).

Another part of using style in a specific context is our *purpose*. A purpose is always present behind our words, even if we are not fully aware of or able to articulate it. Some examples of that purpose are to amuse, to persuade, to inform, or to get someone's attention. Lincoln's purpose was arguably not only to honor the sacrifice of fallen soldiers but also to urge others to keep fighting to preserve the nation. Since our purpose is often inchoate, taking shape as we go along, we may not always anticipate, or intend, the results of our words.

We also sometimes cannot anticipate the consequences of our words because it is difficult to know the *audience*, those who read or hear what we say and respond to it. Any audience likely includes some individuals favorably disposed to what we say, but how about those resistant or opposed to our ideas? Thinking about the audience is one of the most difficult aspects of using language because that group must be constructed from incomplete knowledge. In writing or speaking, it is helpful to think about what audiences need from us at any given moment to understand and follow our meaning. The audience can determine what style we adopt in a specific context.

Saying that style exists in a certain context with a specific purpose and audience is to acknowledge that style is *rhetorical*, or connected to *rhetoric*, which Aristotle (2007, 37) defined as "an ability, in each [particular] case, to see the available means of persuasion." How is style closely allied with *rhetoric*, which, in addition to Aristotle's description as "the available means of persuasion," has also been called *the art of using language effectively*?

For centuries, style has been one of the five canons, or categories, of rhetoric, along with invention, arrangement, memory, and delivery. In addition, style shares with rhetoric a focus on the *effects* of words, which may be identical to, or different from, what we intend them to be. For example, the effects may be to move readers or listeners, to cause them to act, to inspire them, or to make them calm or angry. The effects may appeal to our thoughts or emotions, eliciting a rational or logical response (*logos*), one tied to feelings (*pathos*), or one based on trust in a writer (*ethos*).

However it is defined, the word *rhetoric* itself has sometimes had a negative connotation, or implied meaning, based on the belief that language is being used to manipulate others, to deceive them, or to "slant" the truth. This idea, which may stem from rhetoric's focus on the effects of language, can be seen in phrases like *that's empty rhetoric* or *his rhetoric is over the top.* Anne Curzan (2013) says rhetoric has been tied to "overblown speech, speech that is big words, but maybe not backed up."

Despite these pejorative definitions, however, it's important to remember that all language is used for specific purposes to achieve certain effects; thus, all language is rhetorical. Take the word *rhetoric* itself. When it is used in a negative light, to elicit a particular response from readers or listeners, it is being used rhetorically. Thus, despite the many positive connotations of the word—think, for instance, about the "soaring rhetoric" of presidents Kennedy or Obama—the negative connotations often get more attention. Ironically, those who use rhetoric in a negative light may have only a vague sense of what the term means and might have trouble defining it as one of its connotations, or its implied meanings, or its denotation—its dictionary definition.

■ STYLE AS INSEPARABLE FROM MEANING

The Writer's Style contends that style is not separate from but integral to meaning. Some have labeled style merely ornamental or "the dress of thought" (Quintilian 1921), arguing that it adds only a surface veneer to the underlying meaning of words. This view implies that *how* we say something doesn't really matter—that meaning precedes style, the latter inserted simply as an afterthought. *TWS* asserts, on the contrary, that style and meaning are *inseparable* and simultaneous. While it is true that style can be separated *analytically* from content, that separation making it possible, for instance, to list and explain the stylistic resources in this book, it is equally true that style and content are inseparable in their *operation*. As evidence, consider that the way we say or write something can *itself have meaning*: that is, there is meaning *in* the style—in how we choose and arrange words for certain effects.

An example of meaning existing simultaneously with style, without any operative separation of the two, is the title of Richard Rodriguez's (1995, 756) famous essay "Late Victorians," which uses a *pun*, or play on words, to add layers of meaning. His pun, a trope, refers not only to an architectural style of homes popular in San Francisco's gay community but also to the "late" men who died from AIDS and to the author himself, a "Victorian" by temperament *late* to embrace life. These multiple meanings are possible only through style—the use of a pun—showing that style is not just ornamental or added on to meaning. It is an integral part of meaning itself, the two joined as an organic whole.

▪ TAKE 2

How would Rodriguez's meaning have changed with a title like "Late Victorian Homes"? By adding a word, and possibly clarifying his meaning, he would have removed the title's ambiguity— and its play on words, or pun. The pun adds to his meaning, elevating the interpretation of "Victorians" to signify much more than the homes themselves and of "late" to include a few different connotations. In this instance, in looking at Rodriguez's stylistic choices, one can say that less is more.

▪ DIY

Yogi Berra (2010) is famous for his witty aphorisms. A few examples are "It ain't over till it's over" and "The future ain't what it used to be," and they rely on the colloquial use of "ain't." How are these colloquial expressions an important part of his meaning as well as his style? What difference would it make, for example, if he had said, "It isn't over until it's over" or "The future isn't what it used to be?"

▪ STYLE AS CHOICE

In its close connection to meaning, style involves *choice* since we can always say things in different ways. In this sense, style is a collection of resources available to writers and speakers from the normative, or rule-bearing, resources of a language. French linguist Ferdinand de Saussure (2011) called this overall system "la langue," or language, and, as a part of *langue*, style is a question of the choices we make. Why does it matter *how* we choose to say something?

Consider Scott Russell Sanders's (1995, 734) essay "Under the Influence," in which the author uses "tipsy" as just one of many *colloquial*, or informal, synonyms for *drunk*. He also uses words like "buzzed," "lit up," and "three sheets to wind" but omits a stronger possibility, "annihilated." Each choice of synonym has a different *connotation*, a meaning implied or suggested, that has to do with how we perceive a person's degree of intoxication and, arguably, our attitude toward it.

■ TAKE 2

What does it mean when you meet a new person with whom you spend time, and an acquaintance asks, "Is that a friend . . . or a *friend*?" What is the difference between the denotation and connotation of that word? The first, denotative, use of "friend" makes the relationship seem platonic, while the connotative use implies a romantic relationship.

■ STYLE AS ACADEMIC DISCOURSE

Using style rhetorically is also vital in academic writing, in which we want to find *le mot juste*, the appropriate word or expression, for any occasion and audience. In his oft-cited article "Inventing the University," composition scholar David Bartholomae (1986, 4–5) explains the idea of students learning various academic discourses as "invent[ing] the university for the occasion," much as they might invent, or try on, various writing styles.

> The student has to appropriate (or be appropriated by) a specialized discourse, and he has to do this as though he were easily and comfortably one with his audience, as though he were a member of the academy or an historian or an anthropologist or an economist; he has to invent the university by assembling and mimicking its language while finding some compromise between idiosyncrasy, a personal history, on the one hand, and the requirements of convention, the history of a discipline, on the other. He must learn to speak our language.

In saying that student writers must become insiders, speaking in an academic discourse usually reserved for experts, he suggests that "trying on" academic discourses is much like making various stylistic choices. Style and academic discourse both involve learning to mimic language, working between conventional and unconventional approaches, and both following and breaking the rules.

■ TAKE 2

In "Politics and the English Language," George Orwell (1968, 133) describes what he considers the way modern prose has gone too far. He writes, "I am going to translate a passage of good English into modern English of the worst sort. Here is a well-known verse from *Ecclesiastes*":

> I returned and saw under the sun that the race is not to the swift, nor the battle to the strong, neither yet bread to the wise, nor yet riches to men of understanding, nor yet favour to men of skill; but time and chance happeneth to them all.

Here it is in modern English:

> Objective considerations of contemporary phenomena compel the conclusion that success or failure in competitive activities exhibits no tendency to be commensurate with innate capacity, but that a considerable element of the unpredictable must invariably be taken into account.

■ DIY

In your own words, describe the differences between the passage from *Ecclesiastes* and Orwell's "modern English" translation. Which passage is more effective? Why?

Analyze the style of the passage from *Ecclesiastes*. What are the main stylistic features you notice?

Rewrite the passage from *Ecclesiastes* in your own words, updating it for a twenty-first-century audience.

■ STYLE AS DICTION AND SYNTAX

Why are *diction* (word choice) and syntax (word order or arrangement) so important to the study of style? A writer's decision about which words to use and in what order can have a large effect on meaning. Consider E. B. White's (1995, 537) use of diction and syntax in relating a summer storm in "Once More to the Lake."

> In mid-afternoon (it was all the same) a curious darkening of the sky, and a lull in everything that had made life tick; and then the way the boats suddenly swung the other way at their moorings with the coming of a breeze out of the new quarter, and the premonitory rumble. Then the kettle drum, then the snare, then the bass drum and cymbals, then crackling light against the dark, and the gods grinning and licking their chops in the hills. Afterward the calm, the rain steadily rustling in the calm lake, the return of light and hope and spirits.

In his description, White carefully chooses words like "bass drum" and "cymbals" in comparing the storm to a symphony. Thus, in his diction, he gives the squall human characteristics—that is, he personifies it—asking us to think of thunder and lightning as a musical performance and of the gods as "grinning and licking their chops."

In addition to his unusual diction, especially the use of personification, White is strategic in using syntax, or word order. Normally, a narrative moves forward with verbs. Here, there are a few verbs (e.g., "the boats suddenly *swung*"), but the real action takes place with nouns: "A *curious darkening*," "a *lull*"; "Then the *kettle drum*, then the *snare*, then the *bass drum* and *cymbals*, then the *crackling light* against the *dark*." The nouns, juxtaposed as a list and connected by the adverb "then," dramatize the storm.

■ **Parataxis and Hypotaxis**

White's use of nouns is called *parataxis*, a loose set of syntactical relationships among the elements in his sentences, what the *New York Times* (1981) article "The Private Hemingway," describing Hemingway, calls "the phrases linked by 'and.'" Instead of using subordination, or words that show how the parts of the narrative fit together or rank in importance (called *hypotaxis*), White asks readers to fill in the blanks with the nouns, conjunctions ("and"), and adverbs ("then") he supplies. It is true that the repetition of these conjunctions gives the paragraph a logical sequence, a chronological order often characteristic of hypotaxis. Overall, though, the paragraph consists of unranked sentences, demanding more of the reader to fill in the blanks, and thus it is paratactic.

White also uses the articles "a" and "the" in the excerpt above to move the action forward without verbs. He writes "*a* curious awakening," "*a* lull," "*the* kettle drum," "*the* snare"—and "*the* calm," "*the* rain," "*the* return." The repetition of the articles "a" and "the," presented without other cues, asks readers to supply connections, adding to the paratactic feel of the paragraph. Syntax and diction work together in White's excerpt to make nature itself the center of attention. It claims that importance through *parataxis*.

■ TAKE 2

To think more about parataxis and hypotaxis, consider the arrangement of sentences in the following passage from David Foster Wallace's (1997, 256) "A Supposedly Fun Thing I'll Never Do Again," in which he writes about a journalistic assignment as a passenger on a cruise ship.

> I have seen sucrose beaches and water a very bright blue. I have seen an all-red leisure suit with flared lapels. I have smelled what suntan lotion smells like spread over 21000 pounds of hot flesh. I have been addressed as "Mon" in three different nations. I have watched 500 upscale Americans dance the Electric Slide. I have seen sunsets that looked computer-enhanced and a tropical moon that looked more like a sort of obscenely large and dangling lemon than like the good ole stony U.S. moon I'm used to.
>
> I have (very briefly) joined a Conga Line.

Wallace's sentences are paratactic in nature. There is no subordination, no obvious way in which the sentences are arranged as part of a larger structure. Instead, they all begin in the same way ("I have"), and the reader is left to make connections among the disparate elements found in the sentences.

■ DIY

In the following paragraph from *Borderlands/La Frontera: The New Mestiza*, Gloria Anzaldúa (1987, 33) describes the plight of Mexicans crossing the border legally and illegally. How does she deploy *parataxis* to convey her ideas? Is there any use of *hypotaxis*, or ranking, in her paragraph?

> Faceless, nameless, invisible, taunted with "Hey curaracho" (cockroach). Trembling with fear, yet filled with courage, a courage born of desperation. Barefoot and uneducated, Mexicans with hands like boot soles gather at night by the river where two worlds merge creating what Reagan calls a frontline, a war zone. The convergence has created a shock culture, a border culture, a third country, a closed country.

■ CRITICAL THINKING

■ Academic Discourse

1. In the original version of his article "Inventing the University," composition scholar David Bartholomae (1986, 10) writes about a composition exercise in which students are asked to describe baseball to a Martian: "When students are writing for a teacher, writing becomes more problematic than it is for students who are describing baseball to a Martian." In a revised version of his article, Bartholomae changes "Martian" to "Eskimo." He is discussing the need for student writers to become insiders, with the right to speak in an academic discourse usually reserved for experts. Why is his change of diction (from "Martian" to "Eskimo") important as part of academic discourse? In academic writing, can you think of any other examples of how changing just one word can have an important effect on meaning?

2. Explain your understanding of the following opening to Bartholomae's (1986, 4) article, and state how it applies to the study of style:

> Every time a student sits down to write for us, he has to invent the university for the occasion—invent the university, that is, or a branch of it, like history or anthropology or economics or English. The student has to learn

to speak our language, to speak as we do, to try on the peculiar ways of knowing, selecting, evaluating, reporting, concluding, and arguing that define the discourse of our community. Or perhaps I should say the various discourses of our community, since it is in the nature of a liberal arts education that a student, after the first year or two, must learn to try on a variety of voices and interpretive schemes—to write, for example, as a literary critic one day and as an experimental psychologist the next; to write within fields where the rules governing the representation of examples or the development of an argument are both distinct and, even to a professional, mysterious.

3. After reviewing Lincoln's Gettysburg Address, choose a topic you feel passionately about and write *your own* Gettysburg Address, or Gettysburg Address-like speech, to capture the significant aspects of your topic.

■ Hypotaxis and Parataxis

4. Compare the following excerpts from Richard Rodriguez (1995) and Henry David Thoreau (2016). Does each author use a paratactic or hypotactic style? Why are the passages effective?

RODRIGUEZ: Sunlight remains. Traffic remains. Nocturnal chic attaches to some discovered restaurant. A new novel is reviewed in *The New York Times*. And the mirror rasps on its hook. The mirror is lifted down.

THOREAU: The light which puts out our eyes is darkness to us. Only that day dawns to which we are awake. There is more day to dawn. The sun is but a morning star.

3 Style as Thinking outside the Box

At this point of sustained heat/humidity, I feel like rigatoni—
rather, gigantoni—left to boil too long. Don't sauce me. Just
toss me.

—FRANK BRUNI, TWITTER, JULY 25, 2011

How can approaches to style help us think about everyday language in new ways? What makes it possible to view something we take for granted in a new light? Sometimes style can be associated with approaches that lie beneath the surface or do not come across as immediately apparent. These less obvious ways to conceive of style promote thinking generatively or productively with language. In fact, they are ways style can help us think outside the box.

How is style as thinking outside the box at work in the above July 25, 2011, tweet by *New York Times* columnist Frank Bruni as he reacts to a heat wave in the New York City area? Instead of simply saying "It's hot outside," which readers take as a given, Bruni uses a *simile*, the comparison of two similar things using *like* or *as*, comparing himself to rigatoni, and then to gigantoni, the latter also an example of *onomatopoeia*, in which a word sounds like what it represents. He then uses *isocolon*, or a similarity in length and structure, with "Don't sauce me" and

DOI: 10.7330/9781607328100.c003

"Think outside the box" visual representation

"Just toss me" made more memorable by his use of assonance, the repetition of the same vowel sound, with "sauce" and "toss." These simple sentences, juxtaposed, suggest his energy has been usurped by the heat and humidity.

What are some other ways in which style is a way for readers and writers to think outside the box? Consider the following options.

■ STYLE AS DEVIATION FROM THE NORM

While style is often considered part of a normative system, calling style *a deviation from the norm* allows us to consider a writer's intentional departure from habitual practices. Deviations in style force readers to transcend conventional thinking to see things from a new perspective, subverting normative structures and thinking outside the box.

What happens when we read a writer's style from an era that falls outside our current norms of Standard Edited English? Does it change our ideas when a passage is translated from another language? Even though we often judge language in terms of the varieties and dialects in common practice today, it's helpful to remember that aspects of style exist in all languages, whether we are reading original or translated versions.

In fact, the idea that style is a deviation from the norm sometimes comes about when a well-known phrase, common enough to be a part of our cultural heritage, originates in another language. It is not uncommon that academic discourse, nonfiction, or fiction we encounter every day has been translated into English. Consider, for instance, these Beatitudes from the Bible's Sermon on the Mount: "Blessed are the meek" and "Blessed are the peacemakers." The reversal of the normal word order, the scheme of *anastrophe*, changes the sentences' usual syntax: The meek are blessed. The peacemakers are blessed.

The stylistic reversal thus focuses attention on "blessed," with its repetition at the beginning of several successive clauses, a scheme known as *anaphora*. The frequent repetition of the word elevates the importance of those who are identified as "blessed." Furthermore, by shifting the nouns "the meek" and "the peacemakers" to the *end* of the clause, they receive more *emphasis* (see chapter 10), calling attention to apparently unrecognized, even marginalized, groups (see also "the poor in spirit," etc.).

▇ TAKE 2

Think of how—and why—St. Augustine (1991, 2) deviates from usual word order, or syntax, in this sentence from *The Confessions*, translated from the original Latin:

> Narrow is the mansion of my soul; enlarge Thou it, that Thou
> mayest enter in.

Because the first clause normally would read, "The mansion of my soul is narrow," this inversion of the usual syntax, called anastrophe, makes us focus immediately on the opening word—"narrow"—and how it diminishes the more expansive "mansion" of his soul. Augustine's reversal emphasizes his perceived deficiency, narrowness, and desire for growth.

He heightens that effect with a *metaphor*, an implied comparison between two unlike things: his soul and a mansion. The metaphor helps us picture the writer's enormous potential for change; it is as big as a mansion. Metaphors and other figures of speech often depart from normal speech or writing patterns and fit the definition of style as a deviation from the norm.

Augustine's second use of anastrophe—"enlarge Thou it"—is a more subtle deviation. Normally, the "thou"—or *you*—would not be written but understood from the imperative or command: [you] enlarge it. By reversing the usual syntax, and rearranging words, he incorporates "Thou" to reinforce his plea for intervention in his life. By using "thou" twice, in quick succession, he shows the gravity of his entreaty, and, to add even more emphasis, he employs it again in a new sentence.

> Narrow is the mansion of my soul; enlarge Thou it, that Thou mayest enter in. *It is ruinous; repair Thou it.* (Emphasis added)

In addition to using anastrophe again with "It is ruinous; repair Thou it," Augustine also uses *alliteration* (ruinous; repair), which emphasizes the writer's degree of despair, and *epanalepsis*, the repetition of the same word, "it," at the beginning and end of the sentence, showing the writer's emotional focus on "it," his soul—including, presumably, its degraded state. By repeating it twice at the beginning and end of his sentence, Augustine reveals an apparent obsession with his soul's shortcomings.

■ STYLE AS ATTENTION

Richard Lanham (2006, xi) discusses the importance of style as attention in his book *The Economics of Attention.* Lanham says, "The devices that regulate attention are stylistic devices. Attracting attention is what style is all about." Lanham's unusual perspective is a way to think outside the box. Consider, for example, how Richard Rodriguez (1995, 768) regulates attention through his use of *isocolon*, or similarity in the structure and length of parallel elements, in the following excerpt from "Late Victorians":

> They walked Death's dog. They washed his dishes. They bought his groceries. They massaged his poor back. They changed his bandages. They emptied his bedpan.

The symmetry here implies the regularity with which Death, personified with human characteristics, claimed AIDS victims in the first decade of the disease, its inevitability as regularized as the (short) length and structure of Rodriguez's phrases. Thus, the use of isocolon, combined in this instance with anaphora, the repetition of "They" plus a verb ("walked," "washed," bought," etc.) at the beginning of successive clauses, produces a steady rhythm that seems to normalize the response to the disease.

What other effect does his use of schemes have? Rodriguez's repetition of the impersonal pronoun "they" (anaphora) along with the short, similarly structured sentences (isocolon) gives the impression that there is a community united against the disease. Notice, then, how Rodriguez marshals stylistic features against AIDS, much like troops on a battlefield join to fight an enemy, all called to attention through the regularized style.

■ STYLE AS EMOTION

Of all the definitions of style, the one that has proved most elusive, and, for that reason, is not often discussed, is of style as *emotion*. How is it that feeling enters into style and helps writers think in new ways or outside the box? It enters as individual expression (see the preceding section), as persuasion, and as an incomplete utterance that creates a demand for completion.

■ Persuasion

Words can be used persuasively as an emotional appeal to the audience, known as *pathos*. For instance, in his inaugural address, John F. Kennedy (1961) uses pathos to call Americans to service, appealing to our emotions in *the way* he urges us to get involved.

Ask not what your country can do for *you*; ask what *you* can do
for your country.

In this sentence, the audience's emotions are invoked through
Kennedy's style: his repetition of words in reverse grammatical
order, a figure of speech known as *antimetabole*. The contrast
between the commands "ask not" and "ask," and the emphasis on the word "you," repeated twice in two successive clauses
and arranged in different parts of each, make the sentence's
rhythm rise and fall. The rhythm adds intensity through word
reversal—and underscores the need (for *you*) to act, heightening Kennedy's ability to persuade his listeners and readers.

■ Emotional Form or the Expectation for Completion

There is another way in which emotion is a part of style. It
occurs when a sentence or sentences create an *expectation*, or
demand, for *completion*. Kenneth Burke (1931, 124) calls this
idea of form in writing "an arousal and fulfillment of desires,"
and he goes on to explain that "a work has form in so far as
one part of it leads a reader to anticipate another part, to be
gratified by the sequence." Richard Ohmann (1967, 410) claims
that an incomplete utterance creates various demands for completion because "a sentence, at its inception, raises questions
rather than answering them." Ohmann adds,

> These demands for completion of a sequence are of course
> subverbal; they are the vaguest sort of dissatisfaction with sus-
> pended thought, with a rational process not properly concluded.
> As the sentence progresses, some of its demands are satisfied,
> others deferred, others complicated, and meanwhile new ones
> are created. But with the end of the sentence comes a kind of
> balance which results from something having been *said*.

What happens when we apply Burke's and Ohmann's ideas to
different texts? In the excerpt from Kennedy's inaugural speech,
the first clause—"Ask not what your country can do for you"—
leaves us in suspense, his use of "ask not" making us wait to
know what we should ask *for*: "Ask what you can do for your
country." In this sense, the sentence's form itself invokes an emotional response in that it demands, and achieves, a resolution.

Consider how Burke's idea of style as emotional form works in "The Falling Man," an *Esquire* magazine article about the search for the identity of a man who jumped from the World Trade Center on September 11, 2001.

> They began jumping not long after the first plane hit the North Tower, not long after the fire started. They kept jumping until the tower fell. <u>They jumped</u> through windows already broken and then, later, through windows they broke themselves. <u>They jumped</u> to escape the smoke and the fire; <u>they jumped</u> when the ceilings fell and the floors collapsed; <u>they jumped</u> just to breathe once more before they died. (Underlining added)

In the article, Tom Junod (2003) uses emotional form by creating expectations within and among sentences. He does so primarily through repetition, especially of the words "they jumped" at the beginning of successive clauses and sentences, a scheme called *anaphora*. Anaphora makes readers anticipate the jumping again and again. He also uses *parallelism*, or a similarity in structure, with "they began jumping" and "they kept jumping," as well as the repeated clause "not long after." Parallelism has the effect of reinforcing the tragic act and heightening its impact.

When Junod writes, "They jumped <u>through windows</u> already broken and then, later, [they jumped] <u>through windows</u> they broke themselves," he withholds the use of "they jumped" at the start of the second clause, where it would normally go (see brackets), instead using deliberate omission, called *ellipsis*, to achieve his emotional impact. Ellipsis shifts our focus from the *act* of jumping to the *windows* through which people jumped with increasing desperation, implicitly making us supply the words "they jumped" ourselves and forcing us to feel closer to their experience.

The author's sympathy for the jumpers' plight also disrupts our demand for completion. Their fall, which culminates at the bottom, street level, is not finished, paradoxically, until Junod ends his paragraph at the *top* of the World Trade Center. He uses elements parallel in structure and length, called *tricolon* (because there are three—see (1), (2) and (3) below), to suggest the jumpers' common routes of descent but then abruptly cuts off these symmetrical phrases with *parenthesis*, a deliberate interruption—signaled here by a dash:

> They jumped (1) <u>from the offices of Marsh & McLellan, the</u> <u>insurance company</u>; (2) <u>from the offices of Cantor Fitzgerald, the</u> <u>bond-trading company</u>; (3) <u>from the Windows on the World, the</u> <u>restaurant on the 106th and 107th floors</u>—*the top*. (Numbers, underlining, and italics added)

The use of parenthesis ("—the top")—similar to an aside in a play or poem—subverts our expectations, showing how the building's zenith, the 107th floor, mirrors the bottom, where the jumpers fell, and, ironically, also marks the nadir, or depth, of human despair.

■ TAKE 2

The idea of style as emotional form, with an expectation setting up the demand for completion, can be demonstrated with *antimetabole* (sometimes also called *chiasmus*), which exists not only in the Kennedy speech but also in other well-known phrases. Take, for example,

> When the going gets tough, the tough get going.

Why is it that the reversal of the repeated words makes the phrase memorable here? It's easy for anyone to easily grasp the phrase "When the going gets tough." The word "when" immediately pinpoints time frame for readers, and the expression "the going gets tough" is a common, or colloquial, expression we may have heard before. But what is the effect of the exact repetition of words in a different order?

First, the word "tough" is repeated. In a principle known as *emphasis*, we process new information better at the end of a clause. Then, that new information (the first use of "tough") becomes known information at the start of the new clause, giving us a helpful way to understand the words, sometimes called the *given-and-new contract*. But it is more than that. The phrase "When the going gets tough" creates an expectation for completion, and the sentence is completed in a surprise way through the reversal of words. With that expectation in mind, the clause "the tough get going" makes us realize that this is a response to adverse circumstances.

■ DIY

Analyze the use of style in J. D. Vance's (2016) *Hillbilly Elegy: A Memoir of a Family and a Culture in Crisis* and describe why it is persuasive.

> So, to Papaw and Mamaw, not all rich people were bad, but all bad people were rich.

■ STYLE AS IDENTITY OR INDIVIDUAL EXPRESSION

As we saw in the introduction, one useful definition of style is as a part of *identity* or *individual expression*. The idea, translated from the French (*le style, c'est l'homme même*) as "style is the man," is that a writer's expression is part of their personality and reflects habits of mind. The French aphorism is allied with de Saussure's (2011) idea of *la parole*, or speech. *Parole* is the unique way in which individuals express their ideas as part of their identities. In contrast to *langue*—the totality of expression in a language—*parole* focuses on the individual characteristics of a person's style. Individual expression, or identity, is closely tied to emotion (see the preceding section) and voice (see the next section).

If style is important in the way we think of our *identity* and as a way of self-expression, how do we normally talk about it? What words come to mind when we are asked to describe a writer's style—or our own? What words are used to discuss a writer's style? According to Louis Milic (1966, 124), Ernest Hemingway characterized his own style as awkward, reflected in the writer's assertion that "'in stating as fully as I could how things really were, it was often very difficult and I wrote awkwardly and the awkwardness is what they called my style.'"

In a summer workshop at UCLA, Virginia Tufte (1971, 2–3) asked forty-four English teachers to describe Truman Capote's (1965) style and tone in the opening thirty sentences of his esteemed nonfiction book *In Cold Blood*. Here are some of the words the teachers used, presented below in opposing pairs to show the contrasting ways they labeled his style and tone:

plain / elaborate	formal / informal
general / specific	brisk / meditative
poetic / conversational	crisp / cadenced
colorful / drab	moving / detached
natural / artificial	rambling / compact
dramatic / dispassionate	conventional / unconventional
concise / verbose	easy / pretentious

■ TAKE 2

Tufte (1971, 34) also cites Louis Milic's discussion of the different opinions of various critics of Jonathan Swift, who describe his nonfiction style with such labels as

civilized, clear, common, concise, correct, direct, elaborate, elegant, energetic, graceful, muscular, nervous, ornamented, perspicuous, plain, poor, proper, pure, salty, simple, sinewy, sonorous, strong, and vigorous, among others.

While all these descriptions reflect impressions of a writer's style, the descriptions sometimes (or often) require further explanation or elaboration. *The Writer's Style* attempts to look beneath adjectives like these to analyze how a writer's style achieves specific effects.

■ STYLE AS VOICE

So. You think you've got yourself a good blog post.
You chose your writing style. You knocked out the first draft.
You allowed it to sit for an hour or a day.
Now it's time to edit that bad dog—ruthlessly. So that it has a fighting chance in the trenches.
—DEMIAN FARNSWORTH, *COPYBLOGGER*

Just as style is a form of emotion, it is also tied to the spoken *voice*, as we hear it in conversation. The above excerpt from Demian Farnsworth's January 2, 2014, post on the blog *copyblogger* suggests that voice has to do with listening to the *sound* of words and sentences as they unfold in writing. Voice emerges from a variety of stylistic elements like tone, rhythm, diction, and syntax. It is "what speech can bring to writing," which is Peter Elbow's (2012) subtitle to *Vernacular Eloquence*.

Farnsworth's diction, or word choice, on *copyblogger* includes "so," an informal word often used to open a topic in conversation, as well as other colloquial terms like "knocked out," "bad dog," and "in the trenches." His tone, or attitude toward readers, is coaxing, gently persuading bloggers of the need to do more, like a coach trying to get an athlete to work harder—"*ruthlessly*"—to avoid complacency. The writer uses a sentence fragment—"So that it has a fighting chance in the trenches"—as an after-thought, just as we might add a phrase in speaking to a friend to reinforce our meaning, especially if we think they might not be entirely convinced.

■ DIY

Identify the sentence fragments in the paragraphs below. Why are they used in a description of the effect of the AIDS crisis in Richard Rodriguez's (1995, 768) essay "Late Victorians," which is also a chapter in his book *Days of Obligation: An Argument with My Mexican Father* (Rodriguez 1992), nominated for the Pulitzer Prize?

> Sometimes no family came. If there was family, it was usually Mother. Mom.
>
> With her suitcase and with the torn flap of an envelope in her hand.
>
> Brenda. Pat. Connie. Toni. Soledad.

In writing, even though we do not have all the benefits of face-to-face conversation, we can convey qualities directly related to the sound of our voices. In addition to the features already mentioned, writers use conversational elements like intonation, or a voice's rise and fall in pitch, volume, and texture—called *timbre*—which includes distinctions like mellow, intense, or warm. Voice also includes natural pauses, pace, and accent, which can vary from region to region and person to person.

How does Rich Taylor's (1978, 132) use of *sound* and *voice* work in his account of test driving a sports car?

Eeaassee down on that throttle, gently up on the clutch and throb*throb*throb*throb* off we go in a faint squeal of tire smoke, just the slightest little twitch sidewise. And that's with no gas at *all*. Run it up to two grand in first. Get it all pointed nice and straight down the highway. All lined up. Now. Hold on tight, tense your back muscles and . . . *floor this sumbitch*. Yaaahoo! Shiiift. 4000-5000-6000. Shiift. 100 . . . 120 . . . Shiiift. Yaawoll. Ecstasy.

When words sound like their meaning—the case here with "throb" and "squeal"—the writer is using a figure of speech called onomatopoeia, adding to the writer's voice. In addition to using colloquial language ("Run it up to two grand"; "Yaaahoo"; "floor this *sumbitch*"), as if he is conversing with readers, the writer creates a rhythm that mimics a car being driven: his sentences accelerate ("All lined up. Now. Hold on tight, tense your back muscles and . . . floor this *sumbitch*"), just as the car does, and we sense the car's velocity, or quickness of motion.

His voice also rises and falls in pitch, as his intonation moves in tandem with the shifting gears and with his use of italics ("*throb*" and "no gas at *all*"). The volume also seems to increase with each set of numbers ("100 . . . 110 . . . 120"), yet the writer's voice finally falls at the end with the use of a climactic sentence fragment: "Ecstasy."

Voice thus adds an auditory dimension to style, with rhetorical effects attributed to the sound of the words we hear in sentences and longer stretches of discourse. As blogs, tweets, and other new forms of online writing are used more often in academic writing, we come to associate a writer with their distinctive voice.

■ DIY

Think about *voice* in Harvard professor Radhika Nagpal's July 2013 *Scientific American* guest blog, "The Awesomest 7-Year Postdoc or: How I Learned to Stop Worrying and Love the Tenure-Track Faculty Life." What makes her voice unique? How does her voice come through in the title of her blog, alluding to a famous movie title?

I really wondered how I'd emotionally survive tenure-track, assuming anyone would even offer me the job. So I asked him [a colleague also on the job market]. How did he feel about doing the whole tenure track thing? Having to prove oneself again after the whole PhD experience? The answer changed my life, and gave me a life long friend.

He looked at me quizzically, and said *"Tenure-track? what's that? Hey, I'm signing up for a 7-year postdoc to hang out with some of the smartest, coolest folks on the planet! Its going to be a blast. And which other company gives you 7 year job security? This is the awesomest job ever!"*

In 2004 when I came to Harvard as a junior faculty, I wrote it on my desk.

This-is-a-7-year-postdoc.

I type it in every day. For all seven+ years I have been at Harvard. No joke.

■ CRITICAL THINKING

■ Style as Emotion

1. How does Truman Capote (1965) use style as emotion in his book *In Cold Blood*?

   Like the waters of the river, like the motorists on the highway, and like the yellow trains streaking down the Santa Fe tracks, drama, in the shape of exceptional happenings, had never stopped there.

■ Style as Voice

2. What are the features of James Derounian's voice in his November 14, 2011, blog for the *Guardian* titled "Academic Writing: Why Does It Have to Be So Dull and Stilted?"

   Not to mention time delay. Can it be right or acceptable that in an age of 24/7 communication you submit an article, wait months for feedback and then—in the happy event that the revised work is accepted—the article is finally published maybe a year later. Currency? Relevance? Agency for change? And if it is printed, you then have the issue of it being read by three people and a dog.

4 | Why Style Matters

Thomas Paine (1776) opens *The American Crisis*, a series of pamphlets written in the months leading up to the start of the Revolutionary War, with the well-known sentence, "These are the times that try men's souls." Paine's eight words are often cited as moving and persuasive. Could they also have altered the course of US history?

The Writer's Style argues that style can change our thoughts, attitudes, and actions. In other words, style, or the *way* we say something, matters. How, and why, does style matter to readers and writers? Style can make writing or language relevant in ways that may not be apparent even to the writers themselves. Here are just a few of the often unexpected ways in which style matters to readers and writers.

■ STYLE REVEALS THE WRITER'S TRUE MEANING

Consider how every word Paine writes is needed to understand his meaning: "These are the times that try men's souls." His opening includes a demonstrative pronoun ("these") followed by a form of the verb *to be* ("are"). The two words leave us waiting for what comes next. What comes next—the direct object "the times"—does not help our understanding much. We still ask,

DOI: 10.7330/9781607328100.c004

THESE ARE THE TIMES THAT TRY MEN'S SOULS

THOMAS PAINE

From Thomas Paine's *The Crisis*

what or *which* times? The full answer does not come until the end: "that try men's souls."

Paine thus holds us in suspense, deferring meaning until the end, the definition of a *periodic sentence*, a stylistic choice. By using the form of his sentence to control how we get information, he builds anticipation, every word crucial to his message. Paine's style gives his sentence momentum: one word is linked to the next, his meaning managed from start to finish.

■ DIY

What is the effect of President Barack Obama's (2009) periodic sentence in his first Inaugural Address?

> As we consider the road that unfolds before us, we remember with humble gratitude those brave Americans who, at this very hour, patrol far-off deserts and distant mountains.

■ STYLE MAKES WRITING MEMORABLE AND ENDURING

In *The American Crisis*, which opens this chapter, Paine (1776) begins with eight words we still repeat centuries later.

> These are the times that try men's souls. (Italics and underlining added)

Why do we remember or care about Paine's sentence? The writer commands our attention through his use of *alliteration*, the repetition of the same consonant sounds. For instance, Paine places the soft consonant sounds *th*, in "*th*ese," "*th*e," and "*th*at," and *z*, in "the*s*e," "time*s*," "men'*s*," and "soul*s*," alongside the hard consonant *t* in "*t*imes" and "*t*ry." The effect of the alliteration is to make his words reverberate through the sound of repeated consonants.

While Paine may not have predicted the power of his words, it is undeniable. If anyone doubts how important the *way* he writes the sentence is, consider these possible revisions of his prose from *The Elements of Style* (Strunk and White 2000, 67):

Times like these try men's souls.

These are trying times for men's souls.

Soulwise, these are trying times.

Commenting on William Strunk and E. B. White's revisions to Paine's sentence, William Zinsser (1980, 37) says Paine's sentence "is like poetry and the other[s] . . . are like oatmeal." The changed versions neither sound the same nor have the same effect. They have few, if any, memorable qualities, which, in Paine's version, come from his style.

■ DIY

Write your own version(s) of Paine's sentence, "These are the times that try men's souls." If possible, use alliteration or try to hold readers in suspense until the end (with a periodic sentence).

What is the effect of your sentence on readers?

What makes Paine's sentence memorable still today?

■ STYLE UNCOVERS THE WRITER'S ATTITUDE OR TONE

In Paine's sentence, the writer's style also reflects a kind of defiance toward those who don't support his beliefs. How do we know that? His *attitude toward his subject matter*, or tone, becomes clear from the effects of alliteration in his complete sentence:

These are the times that try men's souls: The summer soldier
and the sunshine patriot will, in this crisis, shrink from the
service of his country; he that stands by it now, deserves the love
and thanks of man and woman.

Paine reveals his attitude toward individuals apparently
lacking revolutionary zeal by using the sibilant, or hissing, s
sound in words like "souls," "summer," and "soldier"; the z
sound in "times," "men's," and "deserves"; and the hushing
sh sound in "sunshine" and "shrink." These sibilants force air
through the teeth, and the repeated hissing sound—much like
when a person is angry or disdainful—seems to scold irres-
olute "patriots." Words condemning fickleness, like "summer
soldier," "sunshine patriot," and "shrink," are also evidence
of his tone.

■ DIY

What can you infer about Kate Knibb's tone in her July 2, 2014,
blog post on *Gizmodo*, "Stealing My Brother's Walkman"? List
the elements that reflect her attitude toward the topic and her
readers.

The Walkman turns 35 today. If you own one still, it is probably
dusty, and maybe moldy, and definitely gross and old. But for a
while, a Walkman was the thing. Especially in my house.

Describe an item you intensely like or dislike, conveying your
true feelings about the item through your written tone.

■ STYLE TRANSCENDS GENRE (AND OTHER) CONSTRAINTS

Drawing on the scholarship of Carolyn Miller (1984), Anis
Bawarshi and Mary Jo Reiff argue that the idea of a genre
goes beyond simply a way to categorize different types of
texts, instead urging us to think of genres "as both organizing
and generating kinds of texts and social actions, in complex,
dynamic relation to one another" (Bawarshi and Reiff 2010, 4).
Every genre contains both options and constraints. For example, the advent of the web- and mobile-based messaging system
Twitter places the constraint of 140 characters on each tweet

sent. While some may see this as a limitation, style provides a way to transcend constraints and amplify options.

Consider, for instance, the widely circulated November 6, 2013, tweet from President Obama on the occasion of his reelection.

Four more years.

Why do these three words make up what is considered one of the top tweets (and one of those most retweeted) of all time? Arguably it is because of their style, which circumvents the constraints of Twitter in several ways.

First, the repetition of similar vowel sounds (followed by the consonant *r*) in "four" and "more," known as *assonance*, gives the words unusual cohesion. Assonance connects the words through sound in a way that goes beyond their meanings alone.

Second, the use of just three words reinforces what has come to be called *the rule of three*, which emphasizes the effectiveness of items that come in threes. The rule is sometimes called *tricolon*, signaling the three-part structure in clauses like Caesar's *"veni, vidi, vici"* ("I came, I saw, I conquered"). The three-word series ("four more years") helps us recall the tweet.

Third, the words constitute a *sentence fragment*, which leaves out subjects or verbs (or both). Why does his fragment work well? In this case, less is more. No words could capture the magnitude of the accomplishment, yet the fragment, while technically violating a grammar rule, is appropriate for the occasion, allowing us to amplify the words with our own associations.

■ TAKE 2

Think about the way Hillary Clinton, in her Twitter post of November 9, 2016, goes beyond genre constraints in a tweet she wrote after her loss in the US presidential election.

To all the little girls watching . . . never doubt that you are valuable and powerful & deserving of every chance & opportunity in the world.

Not only does she address her desired audience directly, but she slows down the pace of her writing and forces us to focus on every word by her repetition of the conjunction "&," the scheme of polysyndeton. She also brings about a less formal, more conversational style through her use of the ampersand symbol ("&"). The use of "&" could also signal her adherence to the constraints of Twitter, with just 140 characters allowed.

■ STYLE EXPOSES A WRITER'S CONFLICTS OR UNINTENDED MEANINGS

In her book *Gift from the Sea*, Anne Morrow Lindbergh (1955, 21–22) evokes the channeled whelk, a sea mollusk whose shell she discovers on the beach.

> I turn the shell in my hand, gazing into the wide open door from which he made his exit. Had it become an encumbrance? Why did he run away? Did he hope to find a better home, a better mode of living?

Lindbergh uses the *rhetorical question*, a question that implies a response, as a stylistic device, asking the audience to consider various options with her, to think through questions she then answers in unexpected ways: "Had it become an encumbrance? Why did he run away? Did he hope to find a better home, a better mode of living?" For her, the shell's journey turns out to be important as a trajectory for her own journey: "I too have run away, I realize, I have shed the shell of my life, for these few weeks of vacation."

Lindbergh's use of rhetorical questions, a trope, allows readers to realize she is making an extended comparison between the life of the shell's occupant and her own life. She is thus able to enhance her meaning. She goes on to explore the temporary refuge of a beach vacation and to distinguish it from her regular life in a busy city. Style is crucial in creating a connection between Lindbergh and her readers: to think through what's at stake, to ask readers to consider the same questions she is asking, and to work through possible answers with her.

Style also works to help both readers and writers discover what's at stake in Joan Didion's (1961, 225) "Goodbye to All That." The author opens the essay as follows:

> It is easy to see the beginnings of things, and harder to see the ends.

Didion's use of opposition here is called *antithesis*, the juxtaposition of contrasting ideas, often with parallel structure. The use of antithesis anticipates the crux of the essay, or what's really at stake: conflicting views of Didion's idealized versus her actual experiences in New York City. She contrasts "easy" and "harder" as well as "beginnings" and "ends," suggesting that the clarity with which we see the start of an experience becomes murkier as we go along. Using parallel words in different parts of the sentence gives force to the opposing ideas, and her syntax moves what she wants to emphasize—that it is "harder to see the ends"—to the end of the sentence.

In addition, as readers, we're able to arrive at Didion's main point more quickly because of another scheme she uses known as *ellipsis*, the deliberate omission of words already obvious from the context. Here, Didion omits the words *it is* before "harder to see the ends," as the brackets show:

> It is easy to see the beginning of things, and [it is] harder to see the ends.

What impact does ellipsis have here? The use of the syntactic device "it is" at the beginning of the sentence creates a sense of anticipation, or expectation, while its omission later in the sentence propels us more quickly to the contrast Didion intends us to grasp (that it is "easy to see the beginnings" but "harder to see the ends"). Ellipsis helps us discover the writer's perception that what comes last is more difficult—and possibly more disillusioning—than what comes at the start.

■ CRITICAL THINKING

1. An *oxymoron* is the juxtaposition of two terms usually considered contradictory, like *bittersweet, open secret,* or *cruel kindness.* What makes an oxymoron memorable? Write down three or four examples of an oxymoron. Briefly state what makes them memorable.

2. Identify the grouping of words, repetition, and alliteration in this excerpt from Paul Monette's (1992, 278) award-winning book *Becoming a Man: Half a Life's Story.* Then, write about their effect on you as a reader.

But the fevers are on me now, the virus mad to ravage my last fifty T cells. It's hard to keep the memory at full dazzle, with so much loss to mock it. Roger gone, Craig gone, Cesar gone, Stevie gone. And this feeling that I'm the last one left, in a world where only the ghosts still laugh.

3. Where is the main idea located in the sentence below from Henry David Thoreau's (2016, 319) *Walden*?

I learned this, at least, by my experiment; that if one advances confidently in the direction of his dreams, and endeavors to live the life which he has imagined, he will meet with a success unexpected in common hours.

- Explain why this use of a periodic sentence is effective.
- Find an example of a periodic sentence in one of your college essays. Write about why it's effective in the paragraph in which it appears.

5 Style Pushing the Envelope

In his preface to *The Order of Things*, Michel Foucault (1970, xv) cites a passage he says profoundly changed his thinking, apparently originating in Luis Borges, who says it is borrowed from a Chinese Encyclopedia, *Celestial Emporium of Benevolent Knowledge*, where animals are defined in the following way:

> (a) belonging to the Emperor, (b) embalmed, (c) tame, (d) sucking pigs, (e) sirens, (f) fabulous, (g) stray dogs, (h) included in the present classification, (i) frenzied, (j) innumerable, (k) drawn with a very fine camelhair brush, (l) *et cetera*, (m) having just broken the water pitcher, (n) that from a long way off look like flies.

In reading the passage, one might ask, what happens when the symmetry we expect in writing is disrupted? What role does style play in what may be a sense of disorder or chaos? How does it work to push the envelope? The meaning of *pushing the envelope* is generally to go beyond established limits, to exceed the boundaries of what's possible, or to be innovative. In the context of language, style pushes the envelope by forcing us to think of words and meaning in new ways—for example, to cast language in a new light, resulting in our reevaluating ideas or considering them in different contexts. How, then, does the example from Foucault push the envelope?

DOI: 10.7330/9781607328100.c005

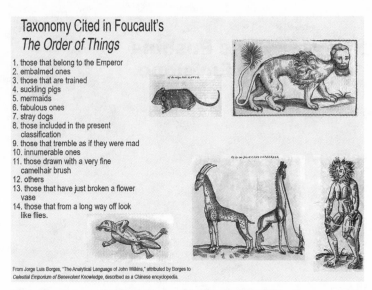

Taxonomy Cited in Foucault's
The Order of Things

1. those that belong to the Emperor
2. embalmed ones
3. those that are trained
4. suckling pigs
5. mermaids
6. fabulous ones
7. stray dogs
8. those included in the present classification
9. those that tremble as if they were mad
10. innumerable ones
11. those drawn with a very fine camelhair brush
12. others
13. those that have just broken a flower vase
14. those that from a long way off look like flies.

From Jorge Luis Borges, "The Analytical Language of John Wilkins," attributed by Borges to *Celestial Emporium of Benevolent Knowledge*, described as a Chinese encyclopedia.

Classification system from Foucault's *The Order of Things*

◼ STYLE DISRUPTS CONVENTIONAL THINKING

The passage from Foucault reminds us that we often think of style as reinforcing ideas through traditional sentence structure or form. Writers sometimes use sentence length or type, repetition, or other means to get meaning across. In the Gettysburg Address, for instance, the last sentence is structured around the repeated phrases "and that government *of the people, by the people, for the people,* shall not perish from the earth." The three phrases similar in length and structure, a form of parallelism known as *tricolon*, are connected to the repetition of the ending phrase "the people," a scheme called *epistrophe.* The symmetry supports his point that people are crucial to self-governance.

In the Foucauldian passage, instead of featuring parallel elements, the list fits what we might call *badly arranged words*, or *ungrammatical, illogical, or unusual uses of language*, a little-known figure of speech, or trope, known as *anoiconometon.* The lack of apparent logic, which may emerge in part from the various languages and translations involved, nonetheless makes us want to find order, patterns, or symmetry in Foucault's taxonomy. The effort to find patterns in disordered elements offers a unique perspective on style.

■ STYLE ILLUMINATES UNSTATED ASSOCIATIONS

Sometimes the most important part of what an author writes is unsaid rather than stated. Style forces us to look *at* the *surface* to help us uncover *what lies beneath it*. Thus, style allows us to "read" *explicit* and *implicit* meanings—not only to look at the words themselves but also to read between the lines. Consider this example from Richard Rodriguez's (1995, 767) essay "Late Victorians":

> The phone rang. AIDS had tagged a friend. And then the phone rang again. And then the phone rang again. Michael had tested positive. Adrian, well, what he had assumed were shingles . . . Paul was back in the hospital. And César, dammit, César, even César, especially César.

The surface of Rodriguez's essay reveals a great deal. By using short, simple sentences (rather than compound or complex ones), he conveys only minimal information. His concise, even curt, phrasing gives the sense of holding back, with a halting, or staccato, effect consistent with the difficulty of describing the horror of the AIDS crisis.

Yet the whole story is told not only in the form of simple sentences. The verbatim sentence "And then the phone rang again" also deploys a trope named *epizeuxis*, the repetition, for emphasis, of a word or phrase in immediate succession. The repeated sentence ("And then the phone rang again") forces us to look beneath the surface and to infer that the phone is likely to ring "again" many more times. Style thus mimics content, the rhythm of the repeated sentence imitating a phone ringing in a monotonous fashion.

When Rodriguez writes, "Adrian, well, what we had assumed were shingles . . ." he ends with *ellipsis*, the deliberate omission of words, suggesting that the unstated disease, AIDS, is more likely than the stated one, shingles. Next he uses a fragment— "And *César*, dammit, *César*, even *César*, especially *César*"—in which the repetition of the same word at the end of successive clauses, known as *epistrophe*, focuses attention on César. César's repeated presence in the sentence makes his absence—his death from AIDS—seem even greater.

■ TAKE 2

Rodriguez (1995, 766) shows how repetition is important in other ways, too. Notice his repetition of the word "absence" in the following lines from "Late Victorians":

> AIDS, it has been discovered, is a plague of absence. Absence opened in the blood. Absence condensed into the fluid of passing emotion. Absence shot through opalescent tugs of semen to deflower the city.

Rodriguez uses a combination of *anadiplosis*, in which the last word of one phrase becomes the first of the next ("absence"), and *anaphora*, or the repetition of the same word at the start of successive phrases (again, "absence") to make the emphasis on absence *present*, ironically calling attention to the destructiveness of AIDS on the San Francisco community. His use of sentence fragments is also appropriate, a way of focusing on absence by showing that the effect of death is to cut off every complete thought.

■ DIY

In Rodriguez's (1995, 767) essay, *how* does he use style to emphasize unstated assumptions?

> If he's lucky, he's got a year, a doctor told me. If not, he's got two.

■ STYLE SHOWS—AND MASKS—THE WRITER'S MIND AT WORK

While we often think of style as following a writer's mind at work, it can sometimes act in the opposite way: betraying a tension authors may not perceive in their own thinking, unaware of what their style reveals. This scenario emerges in Joan Didion's (1961, 233) famous essay "Goodbye to All That," the inspiration for not only the collection *Goodbye to All That: Writers on Loving and Leaving New York* but also a debut feature film produced by

Carlson Sullivan Pictures. In her essay, Didion presents a generally positive account of her experiences in New York City as a young twenty-something without acknowledging the period for what it was—a time of personal failure for her.

> That was the year, my twenty-eighth, when I was discovering that not all of the promises would be kept, that some things are in fact irrevocable and that it had counted after all, every evasion and every procrastination, every mistake, every word, all of it.

On the surface, Didion's style offers a nostalgic recollection, including a few words with negative connotations (e.g., "evasion," "procrastination"), ameliorated by her use of *hedges*, qualifiers like "not all" "some," and "after all," which soften bad perceptions. However, the hedges also reduce her certainty, raising questions about the reliability of her apparent optimism.

Other stylistic features similarly hint at the conflicted nature of Didion's account. She seems to savor her memories, reflected in the way she slows down her prose by reversing normal word order—"That was the year, my twenty-eighth." Yet here the reversal contains a revealing pause, the slower rhythm exposing not only her reminiscences but also the unexpected hint that her time in the city was unproductive. The reversal in this case involves a figure of speech, the scheme known as *anastrophe*.

Didion also repeats "that" to begin a series of successive clauses, the scheme of *anaphora*. Anaphora has the effect of rehabilitating her memories, with each clause, and each use of "that," generating new recollections, each building upon and inseparable from the next, like the layers of an onion. Later, however, the use of anaphora speeds things up, the pace of her memories now intruding: "*every* evasion and *every* procrastination, *every* mistake, *every* word, all of it." The repetition of "every," followed by "all of it," contributes to the accelerated pace.

The same rapid pace picks up even more with her use of *asyndeton*, the omission of the conjunction *and* before "all of it," the omission making it seem as though she is racing to the end. The repetition of the *intensifier* "every" also seems to undermine her case, as though each added use of the word opens a fresh wound. The combined effect of these devices reveals a truth the author seems to want to mask, perhaps unconsciously.

■ STYLE MAKES THE FAMILIAR NEW

While we are accustomed to evocative descriptions of physical locations, style can help us resee things in new ways. For example, E. B. White's (1995, 535) description of a common setting, a summer lake, has qualities at once universal and unique in his essay "Once More to the Lake."

> Summertime, oh, summertime, pattern of life indelible, the fade-proof lake, the woods unshatterable, the pasture with the sweet-fern and the juniper forever and ever, summer without end.

White starts in an unexpected way: by addressing nature, "Summertime, oh, summertime," using the device *apostrophe*, or calling on people or things (present or not) with "summertime." White continues to make the familiar seem unfamiliar by borrowing syntax from a foreign language (e.g., French or Spanish) in which adjectives *follow*, rather than precede, the nouns they modify: "pattern of life *indelible*"; "the woods *unshatterable*." The formal term for this unusual word arrangement is *anastrophe*, a scheme, and the effect of the reversal is to shift emphasis to the ending words, and the enduring qualities, of the experience—"forever and ever."

■ DIY

How does Annie Dillard (1995, 697) make a familiar scene from nature seem new or unique in this sentence, originally from her Pulitzer Prize-winning book *Pilgrim at Tinker Creek* (Dillard 1974)?

> Downstream, away from the cloud on the water, water turtles smooth as beans were gliding down with the current in a series of easy, weightless push-offs, as men bound on the moon.

Write down other examples of authors who make the familiar seem new or unfamiliar in their writing.

■ STYLE VALUES IRONIC OR INDIRECT MEANINGS

While we often seek clarity and direct meanings in writing, it's also useful to use style indirectly to convey our message.

Consider, for instance, why, after a performance that draws a standing ovation, we might turn to a friend and say, "That wasn't half bad." This deliberate use of understatement, a trope called *litotes*, is a form of *irony*, or saying the opposite of what we really mean. Litotes calls attention to the admiration we feel, possibly more than another trope, *hyperbole*, or exaggeration, does, as in, "That was the best thing I have EVER seen!"

The use of indirect or subtle language also allows us to draw on cultural or other associations known to everyone. An example appears in Gary Kamiya's (1996) column on the Sokal Affair, a well-known scandal in which a respected physicist submitted a fake article that was published by the prestigious academic journal, *Social Text*. Kamiya suggests that the hoax was obvious,

> a fact that somehow escaped the attention of the high-powered editors of *Social Text*, who must now be experiencing that queasy sensation that afflicted the Trojans the morning after they pulled that nice big gift horse into their city.

Kamiya enriches his indirect meaning through a *metaphor*, an implied comparison of two things that at first seem unlike: the Trojan Horse and the prank article. The use of the metaphor bolsters the idea of a trick the editors should have anticipated.

His next paragraph consists of just one word:

> Oops.

The use of "oops" as understatement, or *litotes*, resonates in many ways. It refers to a huge controversy that generated discussions around the world. By employing a colloquial way of saying "gotcha," often used when someone is behaving badly, Kamiya brings the highfalutin editors down to the same level as everyone else. Litotes, in the use of the understated "oops," allows us to laugh together about the highly educated editors being fooled by the hoax.

■ CRITICAL THINKING

1. Pick out the use of hedges or intensifiers in the following excerpt from Michael Herr's (1977, 87) *Dispatches*. What is

their effect here? How would the passage be different if he did not use them?

> He was a tall blond from Michigan, probably about twenty, although it was never easy to guess the ages of Marines at Khe Sanh since nothing like youth ever lasted in their faces for very long. It was the eyes: because they were always either strained or blazed-out or simply blank, they never had anything to do with what the rest of the face was doing, and it gave everyone the look of extreme fatigue or even a glancing madness.

2. In the following passage from his essay "Under the Influence," does Scott Russell Sanders (1995, 734) use elements of litotes (understatement), hyperbole (exaggeration), or both? What is the effect of his repetition of synonyms?

> Consider a few of our synonyms for drunk: tipsy, tight, pickled, soused, and plowed; stoned and stewed, lubricated and inebriated, juiced and sluiced; three sheets to the wind, in your cups, out of your mind, under the table, lit up, tanked up, wiped out; besotted, blotto, bombed, and buzzed; plastered, polluted, putrified; loaded or looped, boozy, woozy, fuddled, or smashed; crocked and shit-faced, corked and pissed, snockered and sloshed.

3. Read the following sign described by Edward Abbey (1968, 35) in *Desert Solitaire*, one he supposedly discovered inside a restroom in Utah's Arches National Park. How does he order his list in a way that disrupts our usual ways of thinking? Write down the stylistic elements he uses to change our normal ways of seeing a list.

> Attention: Watch out for rattlesnakes, coral snakes, whip snakes, vinegaroons, centipedes, millipedes, ticks, mites, black widows, cone-nosed kissing bugs, solpugids, tarantulas, horned toads, Gila monsters, red ants, fire ants, Jerusalem crickets, chinch bugs and Giant Hairy Desert Scorpions before being seated.

6 | Style in Sentences

> We hold these truths to be self-evident, that all men are creat-
> ed equal, that they are endowed by their Creator with certain
> unalienable Rights, that among these are Life, Liberty and the
> pursuit of Happiness.
> **—THOMAS JEFFERSON, DECLARATION OF INDEPENDENCE**

We often look at a sentence to understand its underlying meaning. What happens when we go one step further and look at the
way writers use a sentence—a group of words that expresses a
complete thought and includes a noun and a verb—to produce
specific effects? That question is at the heart of thinking about
style in sentences. In this chapter, the question posed is how
does style affect the meaning and reception of sentences among
readers?

■ SENTENCE STYLE IS RHETORICAL

The Writer's Style argues that Jefferson's sentence, one of the
most famous in the Declaration of Independence, and in the
English language, is memorable not only because of its meaning but also its *style*, notably its use of *repetition*, *climax*, and
the *passive voice*, to achieve a specific *rhetorical* purpose. As

DOI: 10.7330/9781607328100.c006

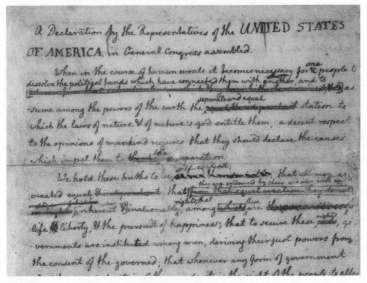

Edited version of the Declaration of Independence

chapter 2 argues, writing is rhetorical when it is based on a specific purpose, context, and audience. How is the style of Jefferson's sentence effective?

The independent clause "We hold these truths to be self-evident" stands alone, as a complete sentence would, but the "truths" he calls "self-evident" become clear only in the next three clauses. Each ensuing clause—a group of words with a subject and verb—starts with the relative pronoun "that." The repetition of "that" at the start of successive clauses, or *anaphora*, connects one idea to the next. The clauses are also arranged in order of increasing importance, a scheme called *climax*. The sentence thus gains momentum, and emphasis, with each new clause.

The sentence also uses the *passive voice*, in which normal word order, or *syntax*, is reversed and a *verb* acts upon its *subject*, as it does in the clause "they *are endowed* [verb] by *their Creator* [subject]." In the *active voice*, by contrast, the verb acts upon its *object*, rather than its subject; as such, the clause would read, "their Creator [subject] endows [verb] them [object]." With the passive voice, the subject can also be *omitted*, as it is in "all men [object] are created [verb] equal [*by their Creator*]." The subject (their Creator) is left out but understood. The rhetorical effect of the passive voice is to shift the *focus* away from the subject (here, the understood-but-absent "their Creator") to the universal ideas Jefferson is articulating; similarly, the *emphasis* (see chapter 10) moves to the *end* of clauses. With the subject—at times called the *agent*—diminished, or absent, Jefferson's principles seem to exist on their own and to be more connected to "all men" than to "their Creator." The use of the passive voice is thus strategic: the independence declared in the document is reflected in its objective, or detached, style.

■ DIY

Identify the use of the *passive voice* in the following excerpt from Martin Luther King Jr.'s "I Have a Dream" speech (King 1963). Why does he use it, or not use it, in the following sentences?

> One hundred years later the life of the Negro is still badly crippled by the manacles of segregation and the chains of discrimination. One hundred years later the Negro lives on a lonely island of poverty in the midst of a vast ocean of material prosperity. One hundred years later the Negro is still languished in the corners of American society and finds himself in exile in his own land.

What other stylistic elements make King's sentences effective?

■ SENTENCE STYLE RELIES ON NOUNS AND VERBS

■ Active Verbs and Verb Style

The active or passive *voice* is related to, but is not the same as, active or passive verbs. (The latter are also known as *to be* verbs.) Conventional wisdom holds that sentences are stronger when we use *active verbs*, like *build, invent*, or *reinforce*, rather than forms of *to be*, like *is*. Active verbs tend to be dynamic, creating a fast pace and moving sentences forward. They can bring sentences to life, endowing them with strength, beauty, and even art.

Consider the use of active verbs in the following paragraph from Hal Borland's (1964, 23) March 31 entry, "Dawn," from his

Sundial of the Seasons: A Selection of Outdoor Editorials from the New York Times, in which he chronicles each day of the year:

> A robin *scolds* in the young daylight, then *sings* a tentative song. Another robin *answers*. A blue jay *flies* to a leafless maple, gray against the sky, and *twitters* a Springsong that hasn't one jeering note. Two redwing blackbirds, fluffed fat against the chill, *talk* hoarsely to each other in a willow whose cautious catkins <u>are</u> still half sheathed. A cardinal *whistles*, *waits*, then *whistles* imperiously as though summoning the sun. Winter's silence *has ended*, but Spring's jubilation <u>is</u> still to come. (Italics and under-lining added)

When we read that a robin "scolds," a blue jay "twitters," or a cardinal "whistles," we get a mental image of the avian ritu-als Borland describes. These active verbs advance us toward the approaching Spring through sounds and movements both harmonious and discordant. The verbs take readers in various directions, creating the impression of a noisy, chaotic season.

■ Passive or To Be Verbs and Noun Style

If the use of active verbs moves the narrative forward, what can be said about the use of the verb *to be* (*is, are, was, were, has been,* and so forth)? Consider the final two sentences of Borland's paragraph, where he writes "cautious catkins *are* still half sheathed" and "Spring's jubilation *is* still to come." In con-trast to the active verbs used to describe the birds, the use of "is" and "are" here suggests a tentative holding pattern, the indef-initeness of time passing. Forms of *to be* are often associated with a less vigorous or static style of writing called a *noun style*. An example occurs in Rachel Carson's (1962, 6) *Silent Spring*:

> The most alarming *of* all man's assaults *upon* the environment *is* the contamination *of* air, earth, rivers, and sea *with* dangerous and even lethal materials. This pollution *is for* the most part irre-versible. In this now universal contamination *of* the environment, chemicals *are* the sinister and little-recognized partners *of* the radiation *in* changing the very nature *of* the world—and the very nature *of* its life. (Italics added)

In the first sentence, instead of using an active verb, as in "man *contaminates* the environment," Carson makes that verb a noun when she writes "is the *contamination* of." Turning a verb into a noun is called *nominalization*. Nominalization often includes the overuse of *prepositions* (here, for example, *of, with, for,* and *in*). Prepositions or prepositional phrases (e.g., "of the radiation/in changing the very nature/of the world—and the very nature of its life") tend to clutter prose and slow readers down. The noun style, with its frequent use of *to be* and its preponderance of prepositions, often uses excessive words and makes writing less concise.

■ Unexpected Effects of To Be Verbs

Just as the *passive voice* can have surprising rhetorical effects, as we saw above in the sentences from the Declaration of Independence and in Martin Luther King Jr.'s I Have a Dream speech, so, too, can the *passive verb to be* (King 1963). While forms of *to be* are usually considered inert, *The Writer's Style* contends that, paradoxically, they can at times seem to have *active* effects related, for instance, to a focus on time elements—the present (*is*) or past (*was*)—or on qualities potentially overlooked: details, images, words, meanings, and rhythms.

In her description of a channeled whelk, for instance, Anne Morrow Lindbergh's (1955, 22) use of *to be* verbs dominates:

> But his shell—it *is* simple; it *is* bare, it *is* beautiful. Small, only the size of my thumb, its architecture *is* perfect, down to the finest detail. Its shape, swelling like a pear in the center, winds in a gentle spiral to the pointed apex. Its color, dull gold, *is whitened by* a wash of salt from the sea. Each whorl, each faint knob, each criss-cross vein in its egg-shell texture, *is* as clearly defined as on the day of creation.

In this *Gift from the Sea* excerpt, Lindbergh uses *to be* in ways that seem incantatory, inviting readers to focus, and reflect, not on what the shell does but on its qualities—simplicity, bareness, and beauty, among others. To highlight these details, she uses *anaphora,* the repetition of "it is" at the beginning of three successive clauses, as well as *tricolon,* the similarity in the length and structure of those *three* clauses—"it is simple; it is bare, it is beautiful." These schemes shape our response through symmetry and rhythm, and her use of a series of *it* clauses (i.e., "it is") shifts the emphasis to the end of each clause.

As the passage ends, she anticipates the use of "is" with *anaphora* and *climax*: "*Each* whorl, *each* faint knob, *each* crisscross vein in its egg-shell texture, *is* as clearly defined as on the day of creation." Anaphora, with the repetition of "each," and climax, with the increasing importance of each successive clause, build to her use of "is," making it stand out and take on added importance. The result emphasizes the shell's physical aspects, with "is" the transition to a comparison of two seemingly unlike things: the shell's architecture and earth's creation.

Lindbergh also uses the *passive voice* in describing the shell: "Its color, dull gold, *is whitened by* a wash of salt from the sea." In this instance, the passive voice has a paradoxical effect by suggesting an *active* process: the shell's dull gold color, gradually whitened by sea salt over time, evokes a natural or organic occurrence. The passive voice thus unveils the process before our eyes, giving it the imprimatur of time, and action, while exposing its ongoing nature.

■ DIY

What effects does Pulitzer Prize recipient N. Scott Momaday (1976, 7) achieve by using the verb *to be* in this passage from *The Way to Rainy Mountain*?

> Yellowstone, it seemed to me, *was* the top of the world, a region of deep lakes and dark timber, canyons and waterfalls. But, beautiful as it *is*, one might have the sense of confinement there. The skyline in all directions *is* close at hand, the high wall of the woods and deep cleavages of shade. There *is* a perfect freedom in the mountains, but it belongs to the eagle and the elk, the badger and the bear. The Kiowas reckoned their stature by the distance they could see, and they *were* bent and blind in the wilderness.

■ Noun and Verb Style Together

Sometimes noun and verb styles and their associated features can work productively together. Consider how they operate in the following passage from John McPhee's (1976, 314) "The Search for Marvin Gardens," listed as one of "The Top Ten Essays Since 1950" by Robert Atwan, founder of The Best American Essays series, on the website publishersweekly.com. The essay is also included in the 2003 collection *Coming into McPhee Country: John McPhee and the Art of Literary Nonfiction* by O. Alan Weltzien and in John D'Agata's 2003 collection, *The Next American Essay*. In the essay, described as "brilliant" by D'Agata, McPhee moves from *Monopoly* game sites to actual, crumbling areas of Atlantic City, which once inspired the board game.

> The physical profile of streets perpendicular to the shore is something like a playground slide. It *begins* in the high skyline of Boardwalk hotels, *plummets* into warrens of "side-avenue" motels, *crosses* Pacific, slopes through church missions, convalescent homes, burlesque houses, rooming houses, and liquor stores, *crosses* Atlantic, and *runs* level through the bombed-out ghetto as far—Baltic, Mediterranean—as the eye can see. North Carolina Avenue, for example, is flanked at its beach end by the Chalfonte and the Haddon Hall. . . . Behind these big hotels, motels—Barbizon, Catalina—*crouch*. Between Pacific and Atlantic is an occasional house from 1910—wooden porch, wooden mullions, old yellow paint—and two churches, a package store, a strip show, a dealer in fruits and vegetables. Then, beyond Atlantic Avenue, North Carolina *moves* on into the vast ghetto, the bulk of the city, and it *looks* like Metz in 1919, Cologne in 1944. Nothing *has* actually *exploded*. It is not bomb damage. It is deep and complex decay. Roofs are off. Bricks are scattered in the street. People *sit* on porches, six deep, at nine on a Monday morning. (Emphasis added)

McPhee changes between noun and verb styles depending on the purpose he is trying to achieve. He begins with a noun style ("is") in his first sentence, using a comparison of two unlike things—streets and a playground slide—to anchor his description. He then moves to a verb style, with active verbs (e.g., "begins," "plummets," "crosses," "runs," "crouch") that depict movement through the neighborhood, suggesting almost frenetic activity.

His return to a noun style offers continuity: "Between Pacific and Atlantic is an occasional house from 1910—wooden porch, wooden mullions, old yellow paint—and two churches, a package store, a strip show, a dealer in fruits and vegetables." His use of "is" positions the neighborhood as historic, one that has "an occasional house from 1910" with accompanying features that might be expected there: wooden porches, yellow paint, churches, a fruit and vegetable stand. Thus, in this case, the *to be* verb suggests longevity and stability.

The pace slows again when McPhee uses a noun style to dwell upon the condition of the neighborhood: "It *is* not bomb damage. It *is* deep and complex decay. Roofs *are* off." The use of "is" and "are" in these simple sentences removes McPhee from the scene; he is a detached observer. The style is reportorial, matter-of-fact, as though the author wants readers to step back, stay removed from the surroundings, and not invest too much in a decaying city neighborhood.

His use of *to be* verbs is followed by the passive voice: "Bricks are scattered in the street." The effect of the passive voice here is to give the impression that the bricks, strewn about haphazardly, are simply part of the landscape. The combination of passive verbs and the passive voice leads to an unexpected final sentence in which the verb "sit," while an active verb, seems *rendered passive* by McPhee: "People *sit* on porches, six deep, at nine on a Monday morning." The active verb suggests inactivity, just as the use of a passive form of *to be* normally would.

■ DIY

How does Jon Krakauer (1996, 199) use noun and verb styles together in this excerpt from his book *Into the Wild*, which was adapted into a feature-length film?

> One of his last acts was to take a picture of himself, standing near the bus under the high Alaska sky, one hand holding his final note toward the camera lens, the other raised in a brave, beatific farewell. His face is horribly emaciated, almost skeletal. But if he pitied himself in those last difficult hours—because he was so young, because he was alone, because his body had betrayed him and his will had let him down—it's not apparent

from the photograph. He is smiling in the picture, and there is no mistaking the look in his eyes: Chris McCandless was at peace, serene as a monk gone to God.

■ LEVELS OF STYLE IN SENTENCES

■ What Are Levels of Style?

When you sit down to write, how do you decide how formal or informal to make your prose? Are the words you choose elaborate or simple? Do they make up long or short sentences? What order do you put words in and where do you place the emphasis in your sentences? For years, speakers and writers have asked themselves these questions when they decide how to reach audiences effectively. Think about telling a friend about a "killer" new movie you have seen. If you were analyzing the film in an English class, would you use a conversational term like *killer* or a more formal word like *poignant* or *captivating*?

Years ago, the Roman lawyer and orator Cicero (1939) addressed questions like these by dividing the stylistic decisions we make into categories he called "levels" or "characters" of style: "grand" (used to persuade), "middle" (to please), and "plain" (to instruct or prove).

The Ciceronian levels of style have traditionally been thought of as hierarchical, moving from "plain" (considered close to everyday speech) to "grand" (deemed the most elevated level). According to S. Michael Halloran and Merrill D. Whitburn (1982, 60–61), this is the conventional view in which all three levels make use of ornamental devices (for instance, figures of speech or periodic syntax) that are not as evident, or are at least subtler, in the plain style.

Halloran and Whitburn oppose this hierarchical view, however, arguing instead that the three styles are "symphonic" rather than associated with "distinct genres of discourse." They explain that

> a well-wrought speech will use all three to orchestrate the audience's response according to the speaker's aim. Plain, middle, and grand styles are levels of embellishment and emotional concentration rather than generically distinct modes of language. (61)

What's important here, as Halloran and Whitburn (1982, 61) claim, is that "stylistic competence consists in the ability to move from level to level, shaping a curve of audience response from intellectual receptivity, to delight, to conviction and commitment."

Richard Lanham (1983a, 161) also proposes a more nuanced view of Cicero's "levels," or "characters," of style, which he renames "high," "middle," and "low." Asserting that "Americans have always had a hard time with the high style," Lanham suggests we have the illusion that anyone adopting it is "fake, putting on the dog, insincere." He goes on to state a parallel illusion we hold of the "low" style: that "down home, plain, folksy, colloquial, ungrammatical = REAL AND SINCERE" (161).

Lanham's main point is that writers often adopt "a balancing act" and end up "translating" between "high" and "low" styles. He cites A. E. Housman, who, Lanham says, "alternates between a formal and a less formal, a higher and a lower, a generally Latinate and a generally Anglo-Saxon style." For example, Housman begins with what Lanham categorizes as the "Latinate or formal" phrase "hunger and thirst cannot be neglected with impunity" and, a few sentences afterward, translates that into what Lanham calls Housman's "Anglo-Saxon and informal" phrase, "a man ought to eat and drink."

Today, the levels, or characters, of style are often integrated or balanced in ways we would consider nonhierarchical. Still, it's useful to consider Ciceronian styles in analyzing prose. In that light, a "plain" or "low" style is often associated with the colloquial, or conversational, uses of language or with teaching, analysis, or providing evidence. A "grand" or "high" style may be used for solemn occasions, like a president's inaugural address or a eulogy. A "middle" style occupies a fluid location between the two. The level of style depends on the purpose, occasion, audience, and context—rhetorical decisions everyone makes, consciously or not, in writing or speaking.

In looking at different levels, or characters, of style, it becomes clear that it's impossible to write *without* style. If you haven't thought much about levels of style, consider what we learn about individuals from their formal or informal style of writing. Can we conclude anything based on *where* we find the writing—for example, in a magazine or a speech, or on Facebook or Twitter? As you read the following examples, think about why writers are using different stylistic levels and how the levels may be "symphonic," to borrow Halloran and Whitburn's term.

■ "High" Style

"High" style is often associated with solemn or ceremonial occasions when we want to persuade or move audiences with words and ideas. Lincoln's Gettysburg Address is an example. What makes style "high" cannot be reduced to any specific characteristics but usually includes formal elements, as in this opening of Barbara Tuchman's (1962, 1) Pulitzer Prize-winning *The Guns of August*:

> So gorgeous was the spectacle on the May morning of 1910 when nine kings rode in the funeral of Edward VII of England that the crowd waiting in hushed and black-clad awe, could not keep back gasps of admiration. In scarlet and blue and green and purple, three by three the sovereigns rode through the palace gates, with plumed helmets, gold braid, crimson sashes, and jeweled orders flashing in the sun. . . . Together they represented seventy nations in the greatest assemblage of royalty and rank ever gathered in one place and, of its kind, the last. The muffled tongue of Big Ben tolled nine by the clock as the cortege left the palace, but on history's clock it was sunset, and the sun of the world was setting in a dying blaze of splendor never to be seen again.

One aspect that characterizes her use of "high" style is starting with a *periodic sentence*, which defers its main point until the end. Most sentences begin with the main idea, but here the main subject and verb do not come until the *last* part of the sentence: "the crowd . . . could not keep back gasps of admiration." The delay in a periodic sentence helps to build anticipation.

In addition, Tuchman underscores the pageantry of the cortege with various details, such as "in scarlet *and* blue *and* green *and* purple." By using the conjunction "and" to separate colors, she makes us slow down and imagine each one individually, a scheme called *polysyndeton*. The effect of the ands is to create a whole greater than the sum of its parts.

Tuchman adds to the solemn atmosphere by repeating the same consonant sound, r—a scheme known as *alliteration*—to emphasize the regal occasion: "Together they represented seventy nations in the greatest assemblage of royalty and rank ever gathered in one place and, of its kind, the last." The academic "high" style is also evident when she uses ellipsis, or deliberate omission, by not repeating the phrase "Together they represented" before she writes "the last." Removing words puts emphasis on "the last" as the end of a sentence—and of an era.

The introduction ends powerfully, as Tuchman uses personification ("the muffled tongue of Big Ben tolled nine by the clock") and metaphor ("on history's clock it was sunset"; "the sun of the world was setting") to accentuate the finality of a historical moment. Giving inanimate objects human characteristics (personification) and comparing seemingly unlike things to show their similarities (metaphor) are important to her narrative. Her use of "high" style thus helps us visualize the significance of the occasion, a rhetorical synthesis of style and meaning.

■ TAKE 2

Susan Sontag (1977, 3) uses metaphor and "high" style convincingly in this excerpt from her book, *Illness as Metaphor*. She makes an implied comparison of illness to things that appear to be of unlike nature—"the night-side of life," "citizenship," and a "passport"—thereby illuminating what they have in common with illness.

> Illness is the night-side of life, a more onerous citizenship. Everyone who is born holds dual citizenship, in the kingdom of the well and the kingdom of the sick. Although we all prefer to use only the good passport, sooner or later each of us is obliged, at least for a spell, to identify ourselves as citizens of that other place.

■ DIY

What makes elements of this passage from Barack Obama's (1995, 294) *Dreams of My Father* a part of "high" style?

People began to shout, to rise from their seats and clap and cry out, a forceful wind carrying the reverend's voice up into the rafters. As I watched and listened from my seat, I began to hear all the notes from the past three years swirl about me. . . . And in that single note—hope!—I heard something else; at the foot of that cross, inside the thousands of churches across the city, I imagined the stories of ordinary black people merging with the stories of David and Goliath, Moses and Pharaoh, the Christians in the lion's den, Ezekiel's field of dry bones.

■ "Low" Style

Even though Cicero thought of "low" style as a way to instruct, it has also come to be regarded more broadly as a conversational or colloquial way of speaking, as the earlier excerpts by Dorothy Allison and *copyblogger* show. "Low" style is often considered rational, logical, sincere, or plain, to name just a few of its normal descriptors. It also tends to exclude figures of speech or complicated sentences.

Given the instructional or conversational aspect of "low" style, writers can seem to be talking directly to readers. This is the case in Rich Taylor's (1978, 133) car review, portions of which we saw earlier in examining aspects of voice and style.

Enough is enough. Take your foot off the gas and let it roll. And roll and roll. . . . This is *it*. I mean, this is IT. Right?

With "low" style, writers might adopt expressions from everyday conversations, as in "enough is enough," "let it roll," and "this is it," repeated with "I mean, this is IT," the "IT" capitalized for emphasis. A conversational question—"Right?"—follows, with yes its implied, and logical, response. The rhetorical question, a trope intended to persuade us of the writer's opinion, can be considered a part of "high" style, showing how the levels of style can be blended.

■ DIY

What makes this personals ad placed online on Craigslist a part of the "low" style of writing?

Not into the bar scene—too many lonely souls. Medium height and weight (have stats), brownish grey hair, 5 o'clock shadow, fu man chu, hazel eyes, strong biceps, 35 inch waist wranglers. Looks ain't bad—have face pics to trade. Don't smoke or drink. Health conscious, work out and lift some weekly, but not a gym rat. No beer belly here.

What does the *style* of this tweet say about police attitudes toward the Occupy Wall Street movement by protesters of income disparity?

#NYPD officer says "Time to take a leak boys, this thing is kicking off at 12" #occupy

Rewrite the tweet as though the officer were writing to (1) NYPD Commissioner James P. O'Neill or (2) Wall Street traders.
Analyze this Tumblr-originating OWS slogan:

We are the 99%.

How do a few words say so much? Why are all the expressions a part of "low" style rather than "high" style?

■ **"Middle" Style**

While "high" and "low" styles are usually considered opposite ends of the spectrum, "middle" style is seen somewhere between the two. It often combines ornamented with plain elements, figurative or literary elements with conversational or everyday ones. According to style expert Richard Lanham (1983a, 186), a "middle" style is "wonderfully easy to read aloud. The voice has at every point natural places to rise and fall" and can have an "acute sense of timing, the feeling for narrative suspense and for climax." Lanham (1983a, 164) situates "middle" style between "high" and "low," which he characterizes with these antithetical elements, among others:

"High"	*"Low"*
rhetorical	logical
emotional	rational
persuasive	informational
ornamented	plain

Latinate	Anglo-Saxon
hypotactic	paratactic
literary	conversational
periodic	loose

In his classic work *Walden*, Henry David Thoreau (2016, 142) adopts what can be considered a "middle" style.

> Time is but the stream I go a-fishing in. I drink at it; but while I drink I see the sandy bottom and detect how shallow it is. Its thin current slides away, but eternity remains.

In Thoreau's adage, "Time is but the stream I go a-fishing in," he uses one of the most common figures of speech, a *metaphor*, to compare two things that at first appear to be dissimilar: time and the stream where he fishes. Along with the metaphor, he uses a colloquial phrase, "I go a-fishing in," leaving us to see his somewhat lofty idea as taking place in a common fishing hole. "High" and "low" elements exist side by side to create an unusual effect, written in "middle" style.

Thoreau helps readers understand his meaning through concrete vocabulary like "drinking," "current," and "sandy bottom," but those words are balanced with more abstract concepts like "time" and "eternity." By juxtaposing transparent ideas with those more opaque or difficult to understand, Thoreau achieves a "middle" style we value years after it first appeared.

Are those "middle"-style qualities present in the following excerpt from Annie Dillard's (1995, 697) essay, originally part of her Pulitzer Prize-winning *Pilgrim from Tinker Creek* (Dillard 1974)?

> Downstream, away from the cloud on the water, water turtles smooth as beans were gliding down with the current in a series of easy, weightless push-offs, as men bound on the moon. I didn't know whether to trace the progress of one turtle I was sure of, risking sticking my face in one of the bridge's spider webs made invisible by the gathering dark, or take a chance on seeing the carp, or scan the mudbank in hope of seeing a muskrat, or follow the last of the swallows who caught at my heart and trailed it after them like streamers as they appeared from directly below, under the log, flying upstream with their tails forked, so fast.

Dillard's sentences rise and fall and build suspense toward a climax. The main clause ("water turtles smooth as beans were gliding down with the current") has free modifiers both *preceding* it ("downstream," "away from the clouds on the water"), where they build suspense, and *following* it ("as men bound on the moon"), where they elaborate on Dillard's idea. The first free modifiers create a rising rhythm; the last ones, a falling one.

In addition, Dillard's use of two similes helps us understand the movements of water turtles. First, her simile comparing the texture of their skin to beans ("smooth as beans") gives us an idea of the turtles' inherent slipperiness, facilitating their ease of travel. The second simile, in which Dillard suggests the turtles' "weightless push-offs" are accomplished "as men bound on the moon," allows readers to visualize photos or films we may have seen of astronauts taking apparently effortless leaps in space, just as the turtles do in the water.

Dillard also uses a "middle" style by personifying the swallows "who caught at my heart and trailed it after them like streamers." Her use of *personification*, giving human-like characteristics to the swallows, is an aspect of "high" style, but she also uses colloquial expressions ("caught at my heart"; "trailed it after them like streamers") that allow readers to make a more personal connection with the writer. In addition, her repetition of the first-person pronoun *I* in the expression "I didn't know whether to trace the progress of one turtle I was sure of," and her ending the clause in a preposition ("sure of"), are also indications of a conversational quality.

■ **Translating Styles**

The levels, or characters, of style have a constantly shifting function. Sometimes, it's useful to think of them as distinct, primarily for classification purposes. It's also true, however, that the levels have been convincingly called *symphonic*, part of an intricate and interwoven stylistic network writers draw from to achieve specific rhetorical effects. Alternating or blending levels of style adds to variation.

For example, in his *Atlantic* article "Is Facebook Making Us Lonely?," Stephen Marche (2012) starts by quoting a study written in a "high"-level academic style and then, in a new paragraph, consisting of one sentence, he "translates" the quote. How are the following two paragraphs different?

> Valuing happiness is not necessarily linked to greater happiness. In fact, under certain conditions, the opposite is true. Under conditions of low (but not high) life stress, the more people valued happiness, the lower were their hedonic balance, psychological well-being, and life satisfaction, and the higher their depression symptoms.
>
> The more you try to be happy, the less happy you are.

By "translating" the "high" style into his own words in the final, single-sentence paragraph, "The more you try to be happy, the less happy you are," Marche clarifies the more complicated academic prose. Is the translated sentence "low" style? He addresses the reader directly ("you") and uses simple diction ("happy"). His writing is informative and plain. At the same time, he uses opposing contrast with "the more" and "the less," giving an aphoristic quality to his sentence. Arguably, then, it's a "middle" style, and the integrated style is effective.

◾ DIY

Consider the following example from President Barack Obama's (2016) commencement address at Rutgers University. How is it a good example of translating styles? Why does it work effectively? Would it have worked as well if it had stopped after the first sentence?

> In politics, ignorance is not a virtue. It's not cool to not know what you are talking about.

◾ TAKE 2

Here are a few things to keep in mind about the levels of style— "high," "middle," and "low"—and how they vary depending on a writer's purpose, occasion, and audience. A "low" style is often colloquial, drawing upon expressions and slang we use in everyday conversations or informal contexts like texting or tweeting. A "high" style may be associated with a formal occasion (like a speech) or may include stylistic features designed to elicit an emotional response from readers. A "low" or informal style, of course, can also draw upon listeners' or readers' emotions. While we often expect "high" and "low" style to exist independently of each other, they may well be juxtaposed or blended for specific purposes in writing. The blending may reflect a combination of informal elements in a specific context. "Middle" style often balances elements from "high" and "low" styles. Its use of broad stylistic resources helps readers understand a writer's purpose.

■ CODE MESHING AND TRANSLINGUALISM

For years, linguists and other scholars have focused on the practice of writers and speakers moving between formal and informal varieties of English in a practice called *code switching*, which depends on the context, audience, and other rhetorical variables. But today, composition scholar Vershawn Ashanti Young (2014, 1–11) and others advocate "blending, merging, meshing dialects" in academic and everyday prose, a process known as *code meshing*, sometimes also called *translingualism* or *translanguaging*, among other terms. Young says code meshing allows "true linguistic and identity integration" and is related to code mixing, or combining "dialects, styles, and registers." He goes on to say that "this technique meshes versions of English together in a way that's more in line with how people actually speak and write anyway."

In calling for writing teachers, students, and, indeed, writers everywhere to recognize the multilingual use of languages throughout the world, several scholars have advocated what they call a *translingual approach*, centered on "develop[ing] alternatives to conventional treatments of language difference" (Horner et al. 2011, 304). Seeing language varieties and differences as "fluid" and as "resources to be preserved" rather than as errors, these scholars ask us to question *all* language practices, including those that seem "to conform to dominant standards," and they call for "*more*, not less, conscious and critical attention to how writers deploy diction, syntax, and style, as well as form, register, and media" (304).

Suggesting that writers today are constantly negotiating language rules depending on differing contexts and needs, Bruce Horner, Min-Zhan Lu, Jacqueline Jones Royster, and John Trimbur state the following principles about a translingual approach to writing:

- Deviations from dominant expectations need not be errors.
- Conformity need not be automatically advisable.
- Writers' purposes and readers' conventional expectations are neither fixed nor unified. (304)

Suresh Canagarajah (2011, 273–80) adds to our understanding of a translingual approach in helpful ways, suggesting, among others, the following beliefs about the practice of code meshing:

- Languages, in continual contact with one another, influence one another.
- The codes drawn upon by multilingual language users are not discrete but exist on a continuum.
- Rather than being "at war with one another," the languages used by multilingual language speakers are complementary and contribute to the writer or speaker's "voice."

As an example of the code meshing Young (2011), Canagarajah (2011), and others describe, consider the following from Gloria Anzaldúa's *Borderlands/La Frontera: The New Mestiza* (1987, 57):

On the gulf where I was raised, *en el Valle del Río Grande* in South Texas—that triangular piece of land wedged between the river *y el golfo* which serves as the Texas-U.S./Mexican border—is a Mexican *pueblito* called Hargill (at one time in the history of this one-grocery-store, two-service-stations town there were thirteen churches and thirteen *cantinas*). Down the road, a little ways from our house, was a deserted church. It was known among the *mexicanos* that if you walked down the road late at night you would see a woman dressed in white floating about, peering out the church window.

In another example of code meshing, scholar Geneva Smitherman (1977, 35) combines varieties of what's commonly called

Standard English or Edited American English (Horner et. al 2011, 303) with African American Vernacular English (AAVE) in describing black semantics:

> Yet terms of racial designation have posed a semantic dilemma to black people from the very beginning. The history of this racial labeling process must be viewed in the context of social, political, and cultural forces. A brief look at that history *can hip us to where Black Semantics is comin from* (italics mine).

Here, Smitherman begins with Standard English but changes to AAVE when she uses the phrase "history *can hip us to where*" and "*comin from.*" What is remarkable here is that Smitherman enlivens her standardized discourse by "meshing" it with vernacular expressions.

In this next example by Smitherman (1977, 1), where is code meshing taking place?

> We have had pronouncements on black speech from the NAACP and the Black Panthers, from highly publicized scholars of the Arthur Jenssen-William Shockley bent, from executives of national corporations such as Greyhound, and from housewives and community folk. I mean, really, it seem like everybody and they momma done had something to say on the subject!

The example of code meshing in the last sentence "*I mean, really, it seem like everybody and they momma done had something to say on the subject!*" comes after Smitherman's use of what is often called Standard English. Smitherman thus uses code meshing strategically to underscore her argument.

Young (2010) also uses code meshing in his response to literary scholar and cultural critic Stanley Fish's three-part series "What Should Colleges Teach?," which appeared in August and September 2009 in the *New York Times* blog *Opinionator*. Young's response aims particularly at part 3 of Fish's articles and Fish's attack on NCTE's The Students' Right to Their Own Language document. Fish writes,

> What would a composition course based on the method I urge look like? . . . I have reached some conclusions. First, you must clear your mind of the orthodoxies that have taken hold in the composition world. The main orthodoxy is nicely encapsulated

in this resolution adopted in 1974 by the Conference on College Composition and Communication: "We affirm the students' right to their own patterns and varieties of language—the dialects of their nurture or whatever dialects in which they find their own identity and style."

Here is Young's (2010, 110) response to Fish, in which he adopts code meshing as the style in which he responds to Fish's claims. Notice the ways in which he combines different varieties of English to help make his point even more persuasive.

Cultural critic Stanley Fish come talkin bout—in his three-piece *New York Times* "What Should Colleges Teach?" suit—there only one way to speak and write to get ahead in the world, that writin teachers should "clear [they] mind of the orthodoxies that have taken hold in the composition world" ("Part 3"). He say dont no student have a rite to they own language if that language make them "vulnerable to prejudice"; that "it may be true that the standard language is . . . a device for protecting the status quo, but that very truth is a reason for teaching it to students."

■ CRITICAL THINKING

■ Identify Code Meshing

1. How does Gloria Anzaldúa (1987, 84) use code meshing in the following example from her book *Borderlands/La Frontera: The New Mestiza?*

> *Nosotros los* Chicanos straddle the borderlands. On one side of us, we are constantly exposed to the Spanish of the Mexicans, on the other side we hear the Anglos' incessant clamoring so that we forget our language. Among our-selves we don't say *nosotros los americanos, o nosotros los españoles, o nosotros los hispanos.* We say *nosotros los mexicanos* (by *mexicanos* we do not mean citizens of Mexico; we do not mean a national identity, but a racial one). We distinguish between mexicanos del otro lado and mexicanos de este lado. Deep in our hearts we believe that being Mexican has nothing to do with which country one lives in. Being Mexican is a state of soul not one of mind, not one of citizenship. Neither eagle nor serpent, but both.

And like the ocean, neither animal respects borders. *Dime con quien andas y te diré quien eres.* (Tell me who your friends are and I'll tell you who you are.)—Mexican saying

■ Comparing "High," "Low," and "Middle" Style

2. How is the following excerpt from Alex Ross's (2007, 113) *The Rest Is Noise: Listening to the Twentieth Century,* in which the author discusses what was seen by some as the end of the Jazz Age in the 1920s, a part of *"middle" style*? To answer that question, make a list comparing aspects of "high" style versus aspects of "low" style.

> By official reckoning, *le jazz* lasted all of three years. Cocteau called it to a halt in 1920, announcing "the disappearance of the skyscraper" and the "reappearance of the rose." That same year Auric explained in the pages of the journal *Le Coq* that his piece *Adieu New-York,* a fox-trot for piano, was his farewell to jazz, which had served its purpose. Auric's new slogan was *"Bonjour Paris!"* By 1927, even Milhaud had lost interest in the mysteries of Harlem. "Already the influence of jazz has passed," he wrote, "like a beneficial storm that leaves behind a clear sky and stable weather."

■ Describe the Writer's Translation from "High" to "Low" Style

3. While "high" and "low" styles are often thought of as the antithesis of each other, it's not uncommon for them to appear together, juxtaposed much as they are in the excerpt below by Salon.com columnist Gary Kamiya (1996). Describe how Kamiya introduces a scholarly quote in a "high" academic style and then follows it with his "translation," using a "low" style.

> It's in his conclusion, though, that Sokal goes over the top and provides some real howlers. "The content and methodology of postmodern science thus provide powerful intellectual support for the progressive intellectual project, understood in its broadest sense: the transgressing of

boundaries, the breaking down of barriers, the radical democratization of all aspects of social, economic, political and cultural life."

Yo! Comrades! Let's go out and transgress some boundaries! And while we're at it, let's break down some barriers! Meet me at noon to radically democratize all aspects of social, economic, political and cultural life! Right after the faculty luncheon at the Regency!

■ Translate from "Low" to "High" Style

4. Try translating this passage from Dorothy Allison's (1995) *Two or Three Things I Know for Sure* from "low" style to "high" style.

> Let me tell you about what I have never been allowed to be. Beautiful and female. Sexed and sexual. I was born trash in a land where the people all believe themselves natural aristocrats. Ask any white Southerner. They'll take you back to generations, say, "Yeah, we had a plantation." The hell we did.

■ Reverse "High" to "Low" Style and Make It "Low" to "High"

5. The following passage by psychologist Jerome Bruner (1996, 151) moves from "high" to "low" style. Try reversing it, starting with "low" style and then moving to "high":

> *Rebus* in its classical sense derives from the Latin *res*, and it denotes how things rather than words can control what we do. Our learned ancestors surely understood the expression *non verbis sed rebus*, explaining in things not words, understanding by doing something other than just talking. Or as the great Ella Fitzgerald put it in a jazzier way, "When you're talking about it you ain't doing it."

7 Style and Generative Rhetoric

Inventing and Elaborating on
New Ideas in Writing

Consider a few of our synonyms for drunk: tipsy, tight, pickled, soused, and plowed; stoned and stewed, lubricated and inebriated, juiced and sluiced; three sheets to the wind, in your cups, out of your mind, under the table, lit up, tanked up, wiped out; besotted, blotto, bombed, and buzzed; plastered, polluted, putrified; loaded or looped, boozy, woozy, fuddled, or smashed; crocked and shit-faced, corked and pissed, snockered and sloshed.
—SCOTT RUSSELL SANDERS, "UNDER THE INFLUENCE"

As a writer, have you ever felt that you have nothing more to say? Have you been unsure about how to expand your sentences or where to go next in your essay? How is it that writers invent or generate new ideas—or elaborate upon ideas that exist in bare form? In the excerpt above from his essay "Under the Influence," Scott Russell Sanders demonstrates one way an author can add on to a simple idea. What do you notice about Sanders's (1995) description of intoxication?

■ HOW TO GENERATE NEW IDEAS IN WRITING

You might have noticed that Sanders's (1995, 734) sentence resembles a list. But how is his list different from, say, a grocery

DOI: 10.7330/9781607328100.c007

David Brooks, "One Nation, Slightly Divisible"

The outdoor guys wear faded black T-shirts they
once picked up at a Lynyrd Skynyrd concert and
wrecked jeans that appear to be washed faithfully at
least once a year.

They've got wraparound NASCAR glasses,
← *maybe a NAPA auto parts cap,* **and** *←haircut
in a short wedge up front but flowing down over
their shoulders in the back—* *←a* **cut known as
a mullet,** *←which is sort of a cross between Van
Halen's style and Kenny Rogers's,* *←and is the
ugliest hairdo since every hairdo in the seventies.*

Representation of David Brooks's sentence using generative rhetoric

list? What do you see in the way he arranges words? Repeats
vowel and consonant sounds? Uses prepositions (like *in* and *to*)
and slang terms?

Sanders's first five synonyms are uttered quickly, with the
chattiness of someone under the influence ("tipsy, tight, pickled,
soused, and plowed"). He then picks up with the one-two punch
of words with similar consonants ("*st*oned and *st*ewed")—the
scheme *alliteration*—or vowel sounds ("j*ui*ced and sl*ui*ced")—
the scheme *assonance*. Sanders also uses synonyms built on
prepositional phrases ("three sheets to the wind," "under the
table," "lit up"), brings in some war metaphors ("tanked up,
wiped out, bombed"), and ends with a few mildly scatological
references ("shit-faced," "pissed").

As readers, how do we normally respond when we see certain
words grouped together? In his long sentence, Sanders changes
between groupings of two ("*s*nockered and *s*loshed"), three
("*p*lastered, *p*olluted, *p*utrified"), and four ("*b*esotted, *b*lotto,
*b*ombed, and *b*uzzed"), and in each group he uses alliteration
when he repeats a different consonant—*s*, *p*, or *b*. His arrangement shows how we might put words together for emphasis. In

this case, the repetition of words, along with the use of alliteration, suggests the excessiveness of a drunk on a bender.

■ DIY

Notice the grouping of words, repetition, and alliteration in this excerpt from Paul Monette's (1992, 278) award-winning book *Becoming a Man: Half a Life's Story*. Think about the effect of these schemes on you as a reader.

> But the fevers are on me now, the virus mad to ravage my last fifty T cells. It's hard to keep the memory at full dazzle, with so much loss to mock it. Roger gone, Craig gone, Cesar gone, Stevie gone. And this feeling that I'm the last one left, in a world where only the ghosts still laugh.

■ CUMULATIVE OR LOOSE SENTENCES

In looking at Sanders's use of punctuation (commas and semicolons) in the excerpt above, notice how they make us pause—or even go in a new direction. Does the arrangement of the sentence have any other effect? The stops and starts (cued by the punctuation) might suggest Sanders is thinking aloud and coming up with ideas along the way. Composition scholar Francis Christensen (1963, 156) says a sentence like this "represent[s] the mind thinking" and claims that most of the sentences we write are based on a principle he calls *addition.*

By addition, he means many sentences are structured by starting with a main clause and then, after that main clause, adding sentence modifiers of varying lengths following the same pattern. The main idea or clause (he calls it a "base clause") appears at—or close to—the start of the sentence (e.g., "Consider a few of our synonyms for drunk"). After that, Christensen adds a series of modifiers (optional words or phrases) he names "free modifiers" since they can be moved freely to different places in the sentence. He says the main idea and free modifiers comprise a "cumulative" sentence (sometimes called a *loose* sentence by scholars like Richard Lanham in his 1983 book, *Analyzing Prose*).

■ GENERATIVE RHETORIC

Christensen calls the entire process of writing cumulative sentences (starting with the base clause and adding free modifiers) "generative rhetoric" because he believes the very form of the sentence can help writers *generate* or invent new ideas. While once a staple in many composition courses, generative rhetoric is not widely discussed today. One reason is that Christensen uses passages primarily from fiction, rarely the basis now for composition courses. Although the *idea* of generative rhetoric may not be widespread, it is at work in some of the best writing we find in different fields. Here is Christensen's (1963, 156) description of the way generative rhetoric works:

> The main clause, which may or may not have a sentence modifier before it, advances the discussion; but the additions placed after it move backward, as in this clause, to modify the statement of the main clause or more often to explicate it or exemplify it, so that the sentence has a flowing and ebbing movement, advancing to a new position and then pausing to consolidate it, leaping and lingering as the popular ballad does.

■ How to Add Ideas to Cumulative or Loose Sentences

To think about how we might use generative rhetoric in writing, consider the following example from *New York Times* columnist David Brooks (2001), whose article about the supposed divide between "red" and "blue" states appeared in the *Atlantic*. In his essay, Brooks distinguishes between men who work either outdoors or indoors. Using the ironic tone characteristic of the whole piece, Brooks begins, "The outdoor guys wear faded black T-shirts they once picked up at a Lynyrd Skynyrd concert and wrecked jeans that appear to be washed faithfully at least once a year." What does the cumulative sentence below add to this? How does it work to generate ideas?

> They've got wraparound NASCAR glasses, ←*maybe a NAPA auto parts cap,* ← *and hair cut in a short wedge up front but flowing down over their shoulders in the back*—←*a cut known as a mullet,* ←*which is sort of a cross between Van Halen's style and Kenny*

Rogers's, ←*and is the ugliest hairdo since every hairdo in the seventies.* (Arrows and italics added)

Notice how Brooks seems to invent the persona of "outdoor guys" starting with the main idea or base clause: "They've got wraparound NASCAR glasses." What happens next? All the free modifiers that follow move backward toward that main idea. For example, the next modifier ("maybe a NAPA auto parts cap") seems almost an afterthought compared to the certainty with which Brooks states that the outdoor guys wear "wraparound NASCAR glasses." Next, Brooks goes beneath the NAPA cap to describe outdoor guys' hair in a series of free modifiers, beginning with "a cut," "sort of a cross," and "the ugliest hairdo." Each one refers back to the base clause, which provides an anchor for considering the subsequent—and cumulative—information.

How else does Brooks's cumulative sentence generate ideas? Christensen says sentences tend to move from general, or abstract, ideas to more concrete ones. In the Sanders excerpt, for example, what role does the word "drunk" serve? It is a general term followed by many colloquial, everyday words for inebriation (e.g., "tipsy," "stewed," and "smashed").

In the Brooks passage, the details he adds about outdoor guys become more concrete (and arguably more gratuitous) with each new free modifier, suggesting that one idea gives rise almost haphazardly to the next. For instance, after describing their hair ("cut in a short wedge up front but flowing down over their shoulders in the back"), he identifies the style as a "mullet" and says it's a cross between the hairstyles of two aging rock and country singers. That leads to his comment about bad hairdos in the seventies. Each modifier thus generates another related idea.

■ DIY

Identify the base clause and free modifiers in this excerpt from Joan Didion's (1961, 235–35) essay "Goodbye to All That."

Discuss what role the free modifiers play in this passage.

How might these stylistic effects be portrayed in a film version?

And even that late in the game I still liked going to parties, all parties, bad parties, Saturday-afternoon parties given by recently married couples who lived in Stuyvesant Town, West Side parties given by unpublished or failed writers who served cheap red wine and talked about going to Guadalajara, Village parties where all the guests worked for advertising agencies and voted for Reform Democrats, press parties at Sardi's, the worst kind of parties.

■ How Generative Rhetoric Works in Periodic Sentences

While generative rhetoric often expands upon the base clause beginning a loose or cumulative sentence, it sometimes works in the opposite way. What is the effect when the base clause comes at the *end* of the sentence instead of the beginning?

While Christensen's main emphasis is on cumulative sentences that start with the main idea, he also says free modifiers that come *before* the base clause, usually in a periodic sentence, move the sentence *forward* rather than backward. How might that work? Consider the following opening of National Book Award nominee Amy Bloom's (2002, 1) essay "The Body Lies," in which she begins her discussion of female-to-male transgender people with an allusion to Kafka's (2016) *The Metamorphosis*. Even though all the sentences contribute to the overall effect, why is her *final* sentence the most essential?

What would you go through not to live Gregor Samsa's life? Not to realize, early in childhood, →*that* other people perceive a slight, unmistakable bugginess which you find horrifying but they claim to find unremarkable? →*That* glimpses of you in the mirror are upsetting and puzzling and to be avoided, since they show a self that is not you? →*That* although you can ignore your shell much of the time and your playmates often seem to see you and not your cockroach exterior, teachers and relatives pluck playfully at your antennae with increasing frequency and suggest, not unkindly, →*that* you might be more comfortable with the other insects? *And when you say, or cry,* →*that you are not a cockroach, your parents are sad, or concerned, or annoyed, but unwavering in their conviction—how could it be otherwise?—*→*that you are a cockroach and are becoming more cockroach-like every day?*
(Arrows and italics added)

Bloom's sentences are all questions, and the interrogative form alone naturally shifts the emphasis to the end of the sentence. But what is the effect of placing the free modifiers *before* the ending main or base clause, "*that you are a cockroach and are becoming more cockroach-like every day*"? As Bloom's paragraph shows, the placement of free modifiers before the base creates *suspense*, forcing readers to hang on every word and, in the process, to experience, with each clause added, the horror of someone feeling trapped in the wrong body. The paragraph is thus *periodic*, with the main idea delayed until the end. By suspending the main idea and building to a climax, each question adds a heightened sense of uneasiness or despair.

How does Bloom's reversal of Christensen's usual cumulative sentence work here? Instead of adding concrete details per se, as we saw in the earlier examples from Sanders and Brooks, Bloom uses *signals* to keep us moving forward. Why does she place those signals here? The repetition of the relative pronoun "that" speeds the sentence toward its climax: ("*that* other people . . . *that* glimpses . . . *that* although . . . *that* you might . . . *that* you are not a cockroach . . . *that* you are a cockroach"). The repetition of "that" at the beginning of successive clauses— the scheme of *anaphora*—creates sentence fragments that tie the questions together, much like the base clause in a regular cumulative sentence does. Bloom uses free modifiers *before* the base to propel us toward her inexorable conclusion about the transgender person's alienation from society.

In the final sentence, when we already know there is some disagreement about the views of the subject's cockroach-ness, Bloom uses the sentence's form to emphasize that tension, ending with the ultimate triumph of the mainstream view. How does she accomplish that? First, by purposely repeating the conjunction "or," a scheme called *polysyndeton* ("And when you say, *or* cry, that you are not a cockroach, your parents are sad, *or* concerned, *or* annoyed"). Bloom's tentativeness seems to say, "It doesn't matter what you do, the result is the same," her repetition, and emphasis, showing the apparent futility of transgender people ever being understood.

Next, Bloom uses *parenthesis*, or interruption ("—how could it be otherwise?—"), as a way to reinforce the idea (in case anyone should question it, she seems to imply) of society's powerful normalizing effect on gender dysphoria.

■ TAKE 2

The scheme of parenthesis is often used as a kind of second thought, almost an aside, to interrupt the normal flow of a sentence. Consider the way it functions in two quotes from a graduation speech at the Massachusetts Institute of Technology by invited speaker Matt Damon (2016). Both uses of parenthesis interject additional ideas to make us think.

> This world, real or imagined, has some problems that we need you to drop everything and solve.

In addressing the idea of simulation theory, Damon asks,

> What if this, all of this, is a simulation?

■ DIY

Where is the main idea located in the sentence below from Henry David Thoreau's (2016) *Walden*?

> I learned this, at least, by my experiment; that if one advances confidently in the direction of his dreams, and endeavors to live the life which he has imagined, he will meet with a success unexpected in common hours.

Write a sentence modeled on Thoreau's in which you state the main idea at the end.

In this excerpt from Richard Rodriguez (1995), which sentence is loose and which is periodic?

> Lonely teenagers still arrive in San Francisco aboard Greyhound buses. The city can still seem, by comparison with where they came from, paradise.

■ Generative Rhetoric in Juxtaposed Cumulative and Periodic Sentences

Is it possible to juxtapose, or place side by side, Christensen's cumulative sentence with the variation of it we saw in Bloom?

An excellent example can be found in the writing of French writer Michel de Certeau (1984, 91), whose widely cited passage from *The Practice of Everyday Life* is translated into English, as many nonfiction and literary texts are, from another language. It begins with his "seeing Manhattan from the 110th floor of the World Trade Center." How does he use generative rhetoric to achieve his purpose?

Beneath the haze stirred up by the winds, →the urban island, →a sea in the middle of the sea, lifts up the skyscrapers *over Wall Street*, →*sinks down at Greenwich*, then →*rises again to the crests of Midtown*, →*quietly passes over Central Park* and finally →*undulates off into the distance beyond Harlem*. . . .

On this stage of concrete, steel, and glass, → cut out between two oceans (the Atlantic and the American) by a frigid body of water, →the tallest letters in the world compose a gigantic rhetoric of excess. . . .

An Icarus flying above these waters, → [the voyeur] can ignore the devices of Daedalus ←in mobile and endless labyrinths far below.

The ordinary practitioners of the city live "down below," ←below the thresholds at which visibility begins. *They walk*—←an elementary form of this experience of the city; *they are walkers,* ←*Wandersmänner,* ←whose bodies follow the thicks and thins of an urban "text" they write without being able to read it. (Arrows and italics added)

Notice that the first three sentences are periodic like Bloom's, suspending the main idea until the end, one of the writer's main patterns. In the last paragraph, de Certeau uses Christensen's cumulative, or "loose," sentences instead, signaling an abrupt change. What accounts for this difference? The type of sentence depends on the vantage point: either high above the city or at street level.

At first, de Certeau's periodic sentences are suspended just as the observer is. The first periodic sentence starts in the air, "flying above these waters" like the mythological Icarus, and finally ends where most walkers do: on the ground in "endless labyrinths far below." Along the way, the use of the periodic sentence gives the up-and-down sense of flight, taking the voyeur, or observer, "over Wall Street" before the observer "sinks down at Greenwich," then "rises again to the crests of Midtown," next "quietly passes over Central Park," and "finally undulates off into the distance beyond Harlem." The rise and fall of the rhythm of the periodic sentence gives the motion of flight experienced by those who observe the city from above.

When he writes from the perspective of the walkers, on the other hand, de Certeau uses cumulative sentences. The main ideas are at the beginning ("The ordinary practitioners of the city live 'down below'"; "They walk"), followed by free modifiers ("*Wandersmänner*, whose bodies follow . . ."). These cumulative sentences thus capture the more concrete process of walking, with the free modifiers giving us additional details about what the city walkers see and feel as they help write the "text" of the city. Along the way, their words, like their walking, generate new ideas almost blindly since, according to Certeau, they can write—but *cannot* read—the urban text they are creating.

■ Using Generative Rhetoric in College Writing

With generative rhetoric, then, it is useful to start by deciding what you want to achieve in your sentences. In Christensen's traditional cumulative sentence, the free modifiers are used to elaborate; in the periodic version we saw in the Bloom example, they are used to anticipate. Both uses are juxtaposed in Michel de Certeau. The direction of modification in the traditional cumulative sentence moves backward toward the base clause (and the main idea). It allows us as writers to add meanings and details we might not have thought of by creating a chain of ideas, one leading logically to the next.

The periodic sentence, which begins with free modifiers and ends with the base clause, moves forward like a narrative, giving readers just enough information to make them want to read more. It delays the overall meaning until the denouement and is effective because it creates suspense, the desire to know more. This variation of Christensen's generative rhetoric thus helps propel readers toward the conclusion and allows writers to invent ideas along the way. Using both forms of generative rhetoric together, as de Certeau does, allows writers to show things from varying perspectives; it also enables readers to experience the way we learn in different contexts.

TAKE 2

How might we sum up the use of generative rhetoric and articulate some of the differences between how it is used in cumulative (or loose) sentences and in periodic sentences?

Generative rhetoric can help us invent new ideas in writing. Cumulative or loose sentences start with a base clause followed by a series of free modifiers. Periodic sentences build suspense by holding the main idea until the end. They work differently from the normal cumulative sentence. Cumulative sentences move backward toward the base. Periodic sentences propel the sentence forward, with the base coming at the end. Cumulative or loose sentences start with a base clause followed by a series of free modifiers. Cumulative and periodic sentences are sometimes juxtaposed by writers to achieve specific effects, like contrasting the feeling of observing a city from above or on the ground. Generative rhetoric tends to resemble the mind at work because it mimics the way we think, stopping to pause (in a loose sentence) or making us anticipate the denouement (in a periodic sentence).

The direction of modification in the traditional cumulative sentence moves backward toward the base clause (and the main idea). As writers, it allows us to add meanings and details we might not have thought of by creating a chain of ideas, one leading logically to the next. The periodic sentence, which begins with free modifiers and ends with the base clause, moves forward like a narrative, giving readers just enough information to make them want to read more. It delays the overall meaning until the denouement and is effective because it creates suspense, the desire to know more. This varied form of Christensen's generative rhetoric thus helps propel readers toward the conclusion and allows writers to invent ideas along the way.

Using both forms of generative rhetoric together, as Certeau does, allows writers to show things from varying perspectives, and it also gives readers the opportunity to experience something in different contexts.

■ CRITICAL THINKING

■ Explain Generative Rhetoric and Rearrange Free Modifiers

1. Explain how the following example from Anne Morrow Lindbergh (1955, 21) works effectively as generative rhetoric. Use terms like *base clause* and *free modifier*.

> The shell in my hand is deserted. It once housed a whelk, a snail-like creature, and then temporarily, after the death of the first occupant, a little hermit crab, who has run away, leaving his tracks behind him like a delicate vine on the sand.

2. Using the same excerpt from Lindbergh, start with "It once housed a whelk, a snail-like creature." Now rearrange the following free modifiers and explain how it changes the meaning of the sentence:
   - and then temporarily,
   - after the death of the first occupant,
   - a little hermit crab,
   - who has run away,
   - leaving his tracks behind him . . .

■ Identify Generative Rhetoric—and Revise the Sentence by Editing Free Modifiers

3. In the following sentence by educational psychologist Jerome Bruner (1996, 119), where is the author's main idea located? How do the other clauses add to his main point?

> A long time ago, I proposed the concept of a "spiral cur-riculum," the idea that in teaching a subject you begin with an "intuitive" account that is well within the reach of a student, and then circle back later to a more formal or highly structured account, until, with however many more recyclings are necessary, the learner has mastered the topic or subject in its full generative power.

4. Now rewrite Bruner's sentence, cutting out the free modifiers you find unnecessary.

■ Revise Sentences Using Generative Rhetoric

5. Rewrite Dillard's (1995, 697) use of generative rhetoric in the two sentences below, substituting your own words to convey the same idea.

> After thousands of years we're still strangers to darkness, fearful aliens in an enemy camp with our arms crossed over our chests. . . . Tremendous action roiled the water everywhere I looked, big action, inexplicable.

■ Analyze How to Use Free Modifiers Strategically in Making an Argument

6. Write about where author Lyle Deniston places free modifiers in a March 2, 2011, post to the *SCOTUS Blog*. What is the effect of using them where he does? How would the passage be different if he placed them in different parts of the sentence?

> In emotional terms, the reaction that is already following the ruling might well be compared with the angry response the Court stirred up when it ruled that burning the American flag, like the Westboro demonstrators' actions, was free speech under the First Amendment, and when it ruled that a march by a band of Nazis through the streets of Skokie, Ill., where many Jews lived, was, like the Westboro protest, shielded by the First Amendment.

■ Combining Elements of "High" and "Low" Style

7. Where do you see examples of both "high" and "low" style in the following excerpt from Michael Herr's (1977, 43) acclaimed work about Vietnam, *Dispatches*?

> Sitting in Saigon was like sitting inside the folded petals of a poisonous flower, the poison history, fucked in its root no matter how far back you wanted to run the trace. . . . A village could disappear in an afternoon [but] Saigon remained, the repository and the arena, it breathed history, expelled it like toxin, Shit Piss and Corruption. Paved swamp, hot mushy winds that never cleaned anything

away, heavy thermal seal over diesel fuel, mildew, garbage, excrement, atmosphere.

■ Use Generative Rhetoric to Describe Nature or a Natural Space

8. In the same manner as this excerpt from E. B. White (1995, 535), write about nature or some outdoor space or setting of your own choice. Use a base clause and free modifiers.

Summertime, oh, summertime, pattern of life indelible, the fade-proof lake, the woods unshatterable, the pasture with the sweetfern and the juniper forever and ever, summer without end; this was the background, and the life along the shore was the design, the cottagers with their innocent and tranquil design, their tiny docks with the flagpole and the American flag floating against the white clouds in the blue sky, the little paths over the roots of the trees leading from camp to camp and the paths leading back to the outhouses and the can of lime for sprinkling, and at the souvenir counters at the store the miniature birch-bark canoes and the postcards that showed things looking a little better than they looked.

8 | Style in Essays, Including Imitation and Digital Rhetoric

Tornadoes, for me, were a transfiguration. Like all serious winds, they were the z-coordinate for our little stretch of plain, a move up from the Euclidian monotone of furrow, road, axis, and grid. We studied tornadoes in junior high: A Canadian high straight-lines it southeast from the Dakotas; a moist warm mass drawls on up north from Arkansas. The result was not a Greek x or even a Cartesian axis but an alchemical circling of the square. Torna-does were, in our part of Central Illinois, the dimensionless point at which parallel lines met and whirled and blew up.

—DAVID FOSTER WALLACE, "DERIVATIVE SPORT IN TORNADO ALLEY"

■ HOW TO GENERATE NEW STYLE IN ESSAYS OR LARGER STRETCHES OF DISCOURSE

While style is often seen in short, contained sentences or para-graphs, it also extends to larger segments of discourse. For instance, when David Foster Wallace (1997) recalls his child-hood of playing tennis in "Derivative Sport in Tornado Alley," a recurring theme is geometry, with terms quantifiable or delin-eated by angles and edges. The essay involves the author's bat-tle between the trigonometric formulas he sees as imposed upon the landscape and the tornadoes that disrupt the "Euclidean

DOI: 10.7330/9781607328100.c008

Illustration of widespread use of Twitter and Hashtags in writing

monotone" of the terrain. How is this constant tension mani-fested in the above excerpt from "Derivative Sport"?

Consider his blending of weather and mathematical nomen-clature. In addition to the use of diction juxtaposing apparently unvarying mathematical elements ("axis," "grid," "square") with similarly monotonous Midwest geography ("furrow," "road," "dimensionless point"), the author uses opposing elements of trigonometry—"z-coordinate," "Greek x." Important to note, Wallace (1997, 8) begins the very nature of his opposition that runs throughout his essay at the start, where he describes the small town in Illinois where he grew up.

> Philo, Illinois, is a cockeyed grid: nine north-south streets
> against six northeast-southwest, dozens and dozens of gorgeous
> slanted-cruciform corners (the east and west intersection-angles'
> tangents could be evaluated integrally in terms of their secants!)
> around a three-intersection central town common.

Here, the disjunction described by Wallace is part of another important opposition: the ebb and flow of the author's own human forces, reflecting the significant decline in his powers as a tennis player. Wallace achieves the effect of highlighting opposition through juxtaposing antithetical elements: a nor-mally regular "grid" rendered "cockeyed"; streets that intersect in divergent directions ("north-south"; "northeast-southwest"); the blending of "slanted-cruciform corners." Through the irreg-ular structure of the essay and the constant shifts in form, he implies a process of constant upheaval, in both the landscape and himself.

Why is this upheaval significant? Wallace's use of geometric shapes offers a contrast between the precision of a grid, on the one hand, and the rolling hills and nonlinear nature of upstate

New York from which the author hails, on the other hand. Style shows how the regular landscape stands in sharp contrast to the cacophonous nature of tornadoes in the Midwest.

■ THINKING ABOUT FORM AND STRUCTURE AS STYLE

Even if we often think of style at the level of sentences, the way larger works are structured, or their form, can reveal a great deal about their style and how it is connected to meaning. For example, think of the structure—and form—of a rejection letter sent to Gertrude Stein in Paris by her editor in New York. Note that Stein was known for her repetitive, often humorous, style, as evident in "A rose is a rose is a rose." In *The Diary of Alice B. Toklas*, Stein (1933, 93) writes, "They moved out and were very comfortable and soon the enormous studio was filled with enormous statues and enormous pictures" and then adds, "That is when he came into Paris to his hour of sketching from the nude, a thing he had done every afternoon of his life ever since the beginning of things, and he came in every afternoon."

In the following 1912 rejection letter from A. C. Fifeld (Farquhar 2015, 153), Stein's editor, how does the form suggest the meaning?

Dear Madam,

I am only one, only one, only one. Only one being, one at the same time. Not two, not three, only one. Only one life to live, only sixty minutes in one hour. Only one pair of eyes. Only one brain. Only one being. Being only one, having only one pair of eyes, having only one time, having only one life, I cannot read your M.S. three or four times. Not even one time. Only one look, only one look is enough. Hardly one copy would sell here. Hardly one. Hardly one.

Many thanks. I am returning the M.S. by registered post. Only one M.S. by one post.

Sincerely yours,

A. C. Fifield

The editor's frustration with Stein's repetition of phrases in her manuscript is shown in the form the letter takes. The writer uses *epizeuxis*, a trope signaling the repetition of the same word or group of words: "only one, only one, only one" and "Hardly one copy would sell here. Hardly one. Hardly one." He also uses the scheme of *anadiplosis*, in which the end of one sentence ("only one") also marks the beginning of the next sentence ("Only one"). What is the effect of these figures of speech on the discourse? Even in such a short space, we see the influence of constant repetition on meaning: it is as if nothing ends—a process of constant beginnings giving the impression that a train has left the depot with no hope of ever arriving at its destination.

The form of the letter is inherently linked to its style. The use of epizeuxis here is paradoxical, with the repetition—ostensibly for emphasis—essentially trivializing the sentiment. The sentence fragment "Not two, not three, only one," which is a use of tricolon—the repetition of phrases in parallel structure—continues the abrupt style, and, when combined with climax, gradually building in importance to "only one," reinforces the editor's overall message that one person can only do, and absorb, so much before being overwhelmed.

These schemes and tropes, though normally a part of "high" style, tend to give the letter an *informal* quality that contrasts with the *formal* nature of the form, a letter, which begins with the salutation "Dear Madam" and ends with the valediction "Yours truly." Indeed, the very form of the letter gives it a formality—a politesse, if you will—that belies (or perhaps ironically exacerbates) the underlying frustration conveyed in the missive.

■ DIY

Consider the following tweets and the importance of form in them. What do you notice happening stylistically?

Oh how I love being ignored. #sarcasm

Thoroughly enjoyed shoveling the driveway today :) #sarcasm

Give other examples of sarcasm in its *written* form—irony.

■ INDUCTIVE AND DEDUCTIVE STYLES

Style works *inductively*, by looking at first-hand examples of how writing operates rhetorically, as well as *deductively*, through logical explanations. The first serves to capture the reader's interest with an anecdote, description, or other details drawing us in without giving too much away. The second offers clear explanations from the beginning, organized logically. One or the other can serve the writer depending on the purposes they hope to achieve. Style is thus useful as a mechanism to negotiate between inductive and deductive approaches to meaning.

Consider the following introduction to a chapter, "February," in Hunter S. Thompson's (1973, 43) *Fear and Loathing on the Campaign Trail.* Do you consider it an inductive or deductive approach to writing?

> It was just before midnight when I left Cambridge and headed north on U.S. 93 toward Manchester—driving one of those big green rented Auto/Stick Cougars that gets rubber for about twenty-nine seconds in Drive, and spits hot black divots all over the road in First or Second . . . a terrible screeching and fishtailing through the outskirts of Boston heading north to New Hampshire, back on the Campaign Trail . . . running late, as usual: left hand on the wheel and the other on the radio dial, seeking music, and a glass of iced Wild Turkey spilling into my crotch on every turn.

In this *Fear and Loathing* excerpt, Thompson describes his rejoining the presidential campaign trail. The passage is highly impressionistic, with details that capture the essence of the writer's state of mind; it therefore leans toward an inductive approach. How does Thompson create that? He does so by offering details of the car ("one of those big green rented Auto/Stick Cougars that gets rubber for about twenty-nine seconds in Drive, and spits hot black divots all over the road in First or Second"), his way of driving it ("a terrible screeching and fishtailing through the outskirts of Boston"), and his state of mind, ("running late, as usual: left hand on the wheel and the other on the radio dial, seeking music, and a glass of iced Wild Turkey spilling into my crotch on every turn"). All are part of an inductive approach.

■ TAKE 2

Thinking back to the use of paratactic and hypotactic style, which one is Thompson using in the above excerpt from his

Fear and Loathing book? Since most of the writing is unranked, without subordination, leaving readers to draw their own conclusions, the passage would be considered paratactic.

■ DIY

How does Thompson (1973, 43) continue his *inductive* approach through the style of the following paragraph from *Fear and Loathing*?

> Not much of a moon tonight, but a sky full of very bright stars. Freezing cold outside; patches of ice on the road and snow on the sidehills . . . running about seventy-five or eighty through a landscape of stark naked trees and stone fences; the highway is empty and no lights in the roadside farmhouses. People go to bed early in New England.

If a writer wants to take a more *deductive* approach, by contrast, how is that reflected in their writing style? Consider the following excerpt from Stephen Hawking's (1988, 65) *A Brief History of Time*:

> Aristotle believed that all the matter in the universe was made up of four basic elements—earth, air, fire, and water. These elements were acted on by two forces: gravity, the tendency for earth and water to sink, and levity, the tendency for air and fire to rise. This division of the contents of the universe into matter and forces is still used today.

In his organized passage, he proceeds logically, using definitions and explanations that lead readers from one idea to the next. Using a cohesive element named the *known (or given)-new contract* (see chapter 10), he ends one sentence with an idea that begins the next—"four basic *elements* . . . These *elements*" (emphasis added). He also twice uses a form of parallelism called *apposition*, a short phrase that serves to explain what precedes it: "gravity, the tendency for earth and water to sink"; "and levity, the tendency of air and fire to rise." He repeats the known-new contract by using concepts he introduced in earlier sentences, "matter" and "forces" ("the division of the contents of the universe into matter and forces is still used today"; emphasis added).

▪ TAKE 2

In his use of a deductive style, Hawking achieves logical associations by using the passive voice productively when he writes, "These elements were acted on by two forces." Here, the use of the passive voice ("elements were acted on by") is in close proximity to the use of "elements" that precedes it ("elements— earth, air, fire, and water") and also juxtaposes the word "forces" with words that define it more precisely: "gravity" and "levity." A deductive style aims to place words so as to achieve cohesion, joining words together in logical, rational ways (see chapter 10).

▪ SHAPE AS STYLE

Style also exists in the shape of words and sentences. The form serves as a bond between style and meaning. For example, notice how student Edward Santos Garza, a student in Advanced Composition, uses vertical lines to describe what happens when David Foster Wallace carefully marries form and meaning in the following passage from "Derivative Sport in Tornado Alley":

> I'd grown
>> up
> inside vectors, lines and lines
> athwart lines, grids—and,
> on the scale
> of horizons, broad curving lines
> of geographic force, the weird topographical drain-swirl
> of a whole lot
> of ice-ironed land
> that sits and spins
> atop plates.

Here is the way Garza (2012) describes the shape of the sentence:

> Wallace constructs sentences that mirror the landscape they
> describe. It is significant that his sentences become longer—
> that is, more fraught with prepositional phrases, parentheses,
> and commas—when he evokes the Midwestern landscape.

Consider again the paragraph's forty-word-long sentence starting with "I'd grown." Whereas two sentences earlier the narrator offers the simple "I'm starting to see why this was so," here he adds thirty-eight words and ten prepositions after the independent clause.

Garza goes on to say more about the shape of Wallace's writing and his use of Christensen's cumulative sentences and free modifiers, writing that "the sentence reveals itself to be like the tectonic plates it refers to, sitting and spinning atop its many prepositional phrases, creating meaning through accumulation." He continues, "Dependent clauses that could have been neatly organized into separate sentences instead swell together. By tacking on these free modifiers, almost recklessly, Wallace creates a sentence as sprawling as the landscape itself."

What, then, can we say about how shape works in a writer's style? As Garza shows, there is often a close relationship between style and meaning, with shape serving as a kind of arbiter, a control mechanism for merging ideas with form, style with meaning. Even if a writer does not consciously think about the shape of their work, the Wallace excerpt reveals that shape is at work under the surface. If we search for it, we can detect shape at work in writing styles.

◼ DIGITAL AND VISUAL STYLE

As examples from Twitter, Facebook, Snapchat, Tumblr, blogs, and other technologies have shown, the advent of the Internet and various digital media has had an enormous impact on what we write, how we write, and the way style and meaning work together. One consequence of these new multimodal tools is arguably an elliptical or telegraphic style based on a more traditionally oral discourse. Many scholars have used the remix model, which relies on the arrangement and juxtaposition of mediums and modes, to describe writing and rhetoric in digital spaces. However, style offers a useful lens for understanding the decisions writers make as they navigate the visual and textual worlds of the Internet using style's extensive resources, from sentences to rhetorical figuration, to understand multimodality in the twenty-first century.

In addition, no one has yet examined new Internet-inflected language phenomena as part of a larger rhetorical theory of style. *TWS* argues that these new language developments are a part of a dynamic elliptical or telegraphic style based on the ironic possibilities inherent in the scheme of ellipsis associated with omission, compression, and economy of expression. Moreover, they are part of a broader evolution of language phenomena made possible by stylistic innovation and are related to the rhetorical canon of arrangement. The impact of a new elliptical style on the practical uses of style and digital rhetoric in composition classrooms illustrates how these Internet-inflected developments have parallels with the field's interest in translingualism, code meshing, and multicultural rhetoric.

These new Internet-inflected linguistic developments are also part of an elliptical or telegraphic style based on the ironic possibilities inherent in the scheme of *ellipsis*. These new elliptical expressions signal a return to implicit meanings, understatement (or *litotes*), and irony, as well as the resurgence of a nuanced, artful online style that borrows from earlier forms of rhetoric.

What are some examples of the Internet-inflected language on style?

■ Prepositional Because

The use of digital media has brought to the forefront the use of the prepositional *because* or the because noun, in which *because* is used in conjunction with a noun to offer an explanation. Consider the following example:

> I am eating King cake for breakfast today. Because Mardi Gras.

Megan Garber (2013), in an *Atlantic* article, "English Has a New Preposition, Because Internet," gives another example, "I'm late because YouTube," and quotes Stan Carey, a writer on language, as saying, ""Because" has become a preposition, because grammar."" As is happening more and more often now in these phrases, an elliptical, or shortened, style emerges, with abridged, even incomplete, phrases taking the place of full, or grammatically correct, explanations.

■ **TAKE 2**

Garber (2013) gives an example of the use of prepositional *because* she found in the *Daily Kos*:

> If due north was good enough for that chicken's parents and grandparents and great-great-great-great-grandparents, it's good enough for that chicken too, damn it. But Iowa still wants to sell eggs to California, because money.

■ **DIY**

Find two or three examples of prepositional *because*. Then write a paragraph from a blog you create with your own use of prepositional *because*.

■ **I Can't Even**

Like prepositional *because*, the phrase *I can't even* often captures thought in a kind of sentence fragment. It is based on the classical trope of *aposiopesis*, "becoming silent," or stopping suddenly in midcourse without finishing a statement. Richard Lanham argues it is "sometimes from genuine passion, sometimes for effect." Lanham (1991, 20) offers a classic example from the scene in Shakespeare's *Henry IV* in which Hotspur is dying:

> HOTSPUR: O I could prophesy,
>   But that the earthy and cold hand of death
>   Lies on my tongue. No, Percy, thou art dust,
>   And food for—
> PRINCE: For worms, brave Percy.

As Slate.com explains, "I can't even" is "an efficient, Internet-inflected way of saying 'I can't even express how I'm feeling right now.'"

An example of *I can't even* appears in the *New York Times Magazine* article "When You 'Literally Can't Even' Understand Your Teenager," in which the author, Amanda Hess (2015), describes "professional fangirl" Tyler Oakley's YouTube reaction to photos of actor Darrel Criss "lounging on a beach wearing only a pair of low-rise jeans and a layer of perspiration." Here is

Oakley's YouTube response to Criss's photos: "'I literally cannot even. I can't even. I am unable to even. I have lost my ability to even. I am so unable to even. Oh, my God. Oh, my God.'"

▇ DIY

Create a 140-character tweet ending with "#I can't even." Be sure to give context for using "#I can't even" in your tweet.

Find two or three examples of the I Can't Even meme on social media (Twitter, Facebook, YouTube, Tumblr, Instagram, etc.). What contexts is the expression used in, and what are the similarities and differences in the uses?

■ Twitter and Hashtags

The advent of Twitter and hashtags has had a marked effect on writing. Given the 140-character limit for each tweet, the technology imposes constraints on its users. These constraints can be useful in learning to write concisely, highlighting the importance of every word in constructing a tweet. In addition, the use of hashtags, and the addition of the symbol # to classify or categorize the accompanying tweet, has contributed to the overall meaning of tweets. Consider, for instance, one of the most celebrated tweets, posted by Adbusters on July 14, 2011, launching the much-used Occupy Wall Street hashtag:

> September 17th. Wall Street. Bring tent. http://bit.ly/
> re9ENL#OCCUPYWALLSTREET

▇ DIY

Write a tweet with a hashtag calling attention to what you consider today's most pressing societal problem or issue.

▇ IMITATION AS INVENTION AND TRANSFORMATION

According to James J. Murphy (1987, xxiii), Roman orator and teacher Quintilian thought of imitation as "the careful following of models until the student is prepared to branch out into his own inventions." Imitation commonly refers to any of a number of practices that range from the verbatim copying of what another writer has composed, beginning with someone else's words and syntax while transforming the subject matter or context, sometimes to achieve *copia*. For classical writer Erasmus (1512), copia meant finding different ways to say the same thing. He produced 195 variations on a single sentence, "Your letter pleased me greatly." Some examples of the same sentences include:

By your letter was I mightily pleased.

I was singularly delighted by your epistle.

Your missive showered a wealth of gladness upon me.

At the sight of your letter the frown fled from my mind's brow.

Your honoring me with a letter was the most agreeable of occurrences.

Pedagogies of imitation that once served as staples in writing classrooms are generally not widely used today, when writing teachers are trying to get students to consider the audience, purpose, context, and occasion of their writing, often as part of teaching argument and analysis—in short, within a specific rhetorical situation.

Quintilian (Murphy 1987, 135) recognized that the practice of imitation is itself changeable and highly rhetorical. In *Institutio oratorio*, he writes, "The first consideration . . . for the student, is, that he should understand *what he proposes to imitate*, and have a thorough conception [of] *why it is excellent*." How can imitation be used stylistically or rhetorically, or how do imitative practices fit into a larger system of style? Knowledge of such a stylistic system would arguably allow writers to extend or expand upon what they are imitating in the process, say, of devising a persuasive argument. Instead of seeming arhetorical—unconnected to the types of writing situations we ask students to take up in our classrooms on a daily basis—imitation arguably facilitates many persuasive rhetorical approaches.

The modern idea of imitation saw a revival in the 1960s, when it had a resurgence based on a renewed interest in classical rhetoric; the hope was that imitation exercises would allow students to emulate certain linguistic and rhetorical features of the author being imitated. That doesn't mean it would be identical; the similarity is of form, not content. There was, of course, the basic method of simply copying a passage. It's also possible to read an analysis of the structure of the model and then compose an imitation. Another is to compose based on models, or the controlled transformation of sentence structures. The idea behind all three is for writers to internalize the structures of the piece being imitated. With those structures internalized, you can make creative choices in your own writing.

Frank D'Angelo (1973, 284) suggests a process for students to imitate models. He suggests they follow a series of steps but acknowledges there may be overlap and variation in the process as students do

> a preliminary reading of the model in order to get an overview of the dominant impression; a careful analysis of the model, which should include quantitative descriptions and a sentence-by-sentence description of the potentially significant linguistic features within each sentence; an interpretation of the passage, including an explanation of the linguistic features and the rhetorical effects; and finally a close imitation of the model.

■ Phyllis Brooks's Persona Paraphrase

In a form of imitation she calls the "persona paraphrase," which involves transforming original passages, Phyllis Brooks (1973, 164) gives students the following instructions:

> Start by substituting words and building a new atmosphere in the passage; you may find that you have to move to whole phrases in order to make your new version of the paragraph understandable. Play around with the words and phrases, but try to keep them in the same order, and the paragraph in the same shape.

To demonstrate her imitation pedagogy, Brooks (1973, 165) quotes a passage from Rose Macaulay's (1966) *The Pleasure of Ruins*.

Once the capital of imperial Rome; later the greatest city in Christendom, the richest city in the world, the spiritual head of the eastern Church, the treasure house of culture and art; then the opulent capital of Islam; this sprawl of mosques, domes, minarets, ruined palaces, and crumbling walls, rising so superbly above three seas, looking towards Europe, Asia, and ocean, oriental, occidental, brooding on past magnificence, ancient rivalries and feuds, modern cultures and the spoils of the modern world, Constantinople has ruin in her soul, the ruin of a deep division; to look on her shining domes and teeming streets is to see a glittering, ruinous, façade, girdled by great, broken, expugnable walls.

To apply the persona paraphrase as a form of imitation, Brooks's (1973, 165) student Leslie Froisland makes the following transformation of Macaulay's passage. It shows the way in which she transformed Macaulay's (1966) original text in her imitation.

[*Bodie, California*] First an assemblage of mining claims; later the largest gold camp in the north, the social hub of all the miners, the place where that shining vein of gold rose up to the earth's surface, the gathering of men in search of fortunes; next the prosperous community, the spread of general stores, town halls, homes that are vacant and drooping fences, sitting so quietly among tall mountains, gazing upon wilderness, nature, and undisturbed lands; silent, solemn, holding gold discoveries and finds, the absence of new inventions and the industry of a modern world, Bodie has death in her future, the death of a useless land; to view her boarded windows and dusty streets is to visualize her glowing past, broken by long, uninterrupted, deplorable solitude.

■ CRITICAL THINKING

1. What is it about these tweets, as sentence fragments, that makes them memorable? Composed by Harry Styles on March 25, 2015, and Louis Tomlinson on October 2, 2011, they are among the most retweeted tweets of all time.

    All the love as always. H

    Always in my heart @Harry Styles. Yours sincerely, Louis

2. Below is a sample passage from Lennard J. Davis's (2001) "Visualizing the Disabled Body." Consider how you might summarize or paraphrase it in your own words.

I have been concentrating on the physical body, but it is worth considering for a moment the issue of madness. While mental illness is by definition not related to the intactness of the body, nevertheless, it shows up as a disruption in the visual field. We "see" that someone is insane by her physical behavior, communication, and so on. Yet the fear is that the mind is fragmenting, breaking up, falling apart, losing itself—all terms we associate with becoming mad. With the considerable information we have about the biological roots of mental illness, we begin to see the disease again as a breaking up of "normal" body chemistry: amino acid production gone awry, depleted levels of certain polypeptide chains or hormones. Language production can become fragmentary, broken, in schizophrenic speech production. David Rothman points out that in eighteenth- and nineteenth-century America, insanity was seen as being caused by the fragmented nature of "modern" life—particularly the pressures brought to bear on people by a society in which economic boundaries were disappearing. This fragmenting of society produced the fragmentation of the individual person.

Following is the way a student used Davis's passage as the basis for her own summary/paraphrase. After reading it, try summarizing or paraphrasing the Davis passage on your own. How is it different from the student work below, and why?

Besides their appearance, people are marked deep inside of themselves. There are people who are emotionally marked from certain events that have happened to them in the past. Also, people who are stricken with an illness or disease are forever marked, but because it remains on the inside, it stays hidden from sight. Disease and illness are a type of inner marking. Lennard J. Davis realized that we are not only physically marked in his article, "Visualizing the Disabled Body." Davis states, "I have been concentrating on the physical body, but it is worth considering for a moment the issue of madness. While mental illness is by definition not related to the intactness of the body, nevertheless, it shows up as a disruption in the visual field" (391). Another example of a disease that has marked not only individuals, but society as well, is AIDS. We are able to view how this disease has marked its victims in Paul Monette's *Borrowed Time: An AIDS Memoir*.

3. Read the passage from Mark Twain's (1996, 455) *The Innocents Abroad* and write your own imitation of the passage. Afterward, read the student imitation of the Twain excerpt from Brooks's (1973) article on the persona paraphrase. How do they compare? What do the differences suggest about the benefits of imitation? First, here is the passage from Twain:

After years of waiting, it was before me at last. The great face was so sad, so earnest, so longing, so patient. There was a dignity not of earth in its mien, and in its countenance a benignity such as never anything human wore. It was stone, but it seemed sentient. If ever image of stone thought, it was thinking. It was looking toward the verge of the landscape, yet looking at nothing—nothing but distance and vacancy. It was looking over and beyond everything of the present, and far into the past. It was gazing out over the ocean of Time—over lines of century-waves which, further and further, receding, closed nearer and nearer together, and blended at last into one unbroken tide, away toward the horizon of remote antiquity. It was thinking of the wards of departed ages; of the empires it had seen created and destroyed; of the nations whose birth it had witnessed, whose progress it had watched, whose annihilation it had noted; of the job and sorrow, the life and death, the grandeur and decay, of five thousand slow revolving years. It was the type of an attribute of man—of a faculty of his heart and brain. It was memory—retrospection—wrought into visible, tangible form. All who knew what pathos there is in memories of days that are accomplished and faces that have vanished—albeit only

a trifling score of years gone by—will have some appreciation of the pathos that dwells in these grave eyes that
look so steadfastly back upon the things they knew before
History was born.

Here is the student's imitation of Twain's passage. Be sure to
try your own imitation before reading what Phyllis Brooks's
(1973, 166) student, Craig Weintraub, writes below.

[*A College Dorm*] After a lifetime of anticipation, it loomed
before me. The tall structure was so cold, so bleak, so
lonesome, so much without any personality or charac-
ter of its own. There was nothing unique in it at all, and
inside on the tile floor were heel marks of all the students
who had been there before. The building wasn't human,
but it wanted to speak. IF the appearance of a building
was ever trying to give a warning, then it was this building
that was philosophizing. It was talking to me, yet also
to others—others who would soon enter its halls. It was
thinking of all that it had seen from the present to the
past. It was fascinated by the movie of its memories—of all
the single frames and incidents which, one by one, quickly
add up till they produce a moving image. It was thinking
of all the people who had come in wanting to make the
world better; of all the idealism and romanticism that had
once flourished; of the individuals with such questioning
minds, whose regression it had watched, whose decay was
observed; of the beginning and the end, hope and death,
the illusions and reality, of all the people who had ended
up as they did not originally want to. It was a lesson
to Man—of the meaning of hypocrisy. It was memory—
knowledge—brought into reality. All those who have a
conception of life—who can easily realize what message
is being conveyed—will realize what the warning is—for
experience has told this college dorm that people who
enter with young and optimistic ideas leave with old and
rational realizations.

9 | Correctness, Clarity, Concision, and Sentence Combining

Style rules . . . are, of course, somewhat a matter of individual preference, and even the established rules of grammar are open to challenge.

—E. B. WHITE, "INTRODUCTION," *THE ELEMENTS OF STYLE*

The study of style has often been connected with language correctness, emphasizing errors and *rules* of grammar and usage. In the introduction to *The Elements of Style*, E. B. White acknowledges the problem with rigid adherence to rules and correctness (Strunk and White 2000 [1979], xvii). Remembering his former mentor, William Strunk Jr., in connection with style, White writes, "Professor Strunk, although one of the most inflexible and choosy of men, was quick to acknowledge the fallacy of inflexibility and the danger of doctrine."

Beyond correctness, the problem of clarity in writing has been an important consideration since the days of Aristotle. More recently, ideas about writing concisely and about the rhetorical practice of sentence combining have been associated closely with matters of style.

DOI: 10.7330/9781607328100.c009

Variation on Standard Edited English

■ CORRECTNESS

Style is often thought of as making language come alive, partly because it uses words in unusual ways. At the same time, language is based on a system of grammar rules, and we generally adhere to those rules when we write or speak. A contrast exists, then, between what we call *grammar*, sometimes referred to as the *ordinary* use of language, and style, the *extraordinary* use of language. In truth, style and grammar operate in mutually informing ways when we write. In fact, style can be seen as a matter of knowing when it's appropriate to observe rules of grammar and usage—and when it's appropriate to circumvent or subvert them.

Because of the operation of a normative, rule-bearing language system, what Ferdinand de Saussure (2011) called *langue*, some writers and speakers try to adhere strictly to rules that have been set down for many years. This idea underlies the concept of *correctness* in language, suggesting there is just one right way of saying something, based on a set of prescribed rules, and there should never be any deviation from that way of writing or speaking. This idea of correctness does not make allowances for social or cultural changes in the way language evolves over time.

The issue of linguistic correctness, of course, is not exclusive to the United States. The French care so passionately about adhering to linguistic purity that they have created the Académie Française to rule on proposed language changes. Often seen as protectionist in language matters, the French Academy recently banned the use of the Twitter term *hashtag*, mandating instead the use of the French term *mot-dièse*, which can be translated as "sharp word" in English.

■ TAKE 2

The French Academy has had similar debates in the past. For example, the group banned the use of the word *e-mail*, adopting instead *courriel*, a fusion of the longer French term *courrier électronique*. The French act frequently to prevent the intrusion of English into the French language, a violation they call "Franglais," or a mixture of French and English words.

A similar fate met the now-obsolete stereo headphone known as the Walkman. The French had dubbed it "le Walkman" until L'Alliance Francaise stepped in to rename it *le balladeur*. Financial penalties were threatened for anyone using the "Franglais" version.

■ Correctness and Language Change

While we do not have a group equivalent to the French Academy in the United States, the issue of language change is a common subject of discussion. Disagreements often arise between those who feel language should not change—and should observe prescribed rules—and those who believe language is always evolving based on significant social or cultural shifts. The latter group, including many linguists, believes language is descriptive and changes naturally—and acceptably—over time.

At the same time, composition scholars like Keith Gilyard (1991) and educational innovator Lisa Delpit (1995) argue that teaching nonstandard deviations makes sense as long as they are taught alongside Standard Written English (SWE), giving students the advantages that accompany the mastery of the English language they need in the business world or in other aspects of their lives.

How does the issue of correctness arise as a matter of style in writing? Consider the following account of Nicola Sacco, an Italian immigrant who, along with Bartolomeo Vanzetti, was convicted of murdering two people in a shoe factory in a widely publicized and controversial case. In its era, the case was as famous as the murder trial of O. J. Simpson. After Sacco's conviction and death sentence, and one month before his execution, he wrote to Pat Jackson, a *Boston Globe* reporter who handled public relations in trying to exonerate him. The account is in Murray Kempton's (1955, 43) *Part of Our Time: Some Ruins and Monuments of the Thirties.*

> We are one heart, but unfortunately we represent two different class. . . . But, whenever the heart of one of the upper class join with the exploited workers for the struggle of the right in the human feeling is the feel of an spontaneous attraction and brotherly love to one another.

Are Sacco's sentences grammatically correct? No, at least not for the most part, and if we are judging the writing by a strict standard of correctness, we might point out the lack of agreement of nouns and verbs; the misuse of articles ("an" where it should be *a*; using "the" where a definite article is not used in English); and the overuse of prepositions, what we previously called a *nominal style.* In fact, if measured by a standard of correctness, the passage falls short in many ways.

Despite its lack of grammatical correctness, why does the passage have such a powerful effect on readers? The writer's style moves readers in various ways. First, Sacco uses the scheme of antithesis, contrasting "one heart" and "two different class," emphasizing what unites the men by juxtaposing "one" and "two" as well as "heart" and "[social] class." He goes on to use synecdoche, substituting the part (the journalist's heart) for the whole (the journalist's body) and thereby placing emphasis on the commonality of *feeling* between the journalist and the oppressed defendants he tried to help. Note that he uses *polyptoton* with the words "feeling" and "feel," using the similar roots to highlight the emotional aspect of their "brotherly love."

■ **Correctness as a Rhetorical Concept**

Even though the sentences fall short on grammatical correctness, the Sacco passage is a stylistic tour de force and demonstrates the idea that correctness is rhetorical. In other words, writing or speaking cannot be judged by strictly applying correctness as a litmus test; instead, the effectiveness depends on the context, purpose, audience, and the words' effects. Since the criminal case generated enormous sympathy for the defendants as well as calls to reverse their death sentence—and then, after their death, to exonerate them—it is important to ask: can the lack of correctness here, perhaps paradoxically, be considered a salutary force?

The idea of incorrectness as positive may seem counterintuitive, and *TWS* is not suggesting that correctness is unimportant. In fact, it is a critical goal we strive for in writing and speaking, and the attention we accord it tends to be a dirty little secret among English teachers everywhere. Yet it is also important to remember that all language is rhetorical. Take popular cultural expressions like *You ain't seen nothing yet* or *Say it ain't so, Joe*, both technically incorrect according to grammatical rules. Despite the nonstandard nature of *ain't*, its use in these examples supplies a perfect stylistic effect for the occasion and fits the definition of style as a deviation from the norm. It captures a nonstandard sentiment, adding an emphatic, almost defiant, note and tone.

◼ CLARITY

In addition to the idea of correctness, it is important to say a few words about clarity as an element of style. What is the relationship of clarity to writing, and how important is it when we are communicating with readers? While the answer might seem obvious to most, it is also true that the idea of clarity has been contested and controversial over time, and it is helpful to examine some of the different ways in which the concept has been approached.

What is the idea of clarity we most want to explore? It probably won't be surprising that the idea of clarity is also rhetorical in the sense that it depends on the context, purpose, and audience as well as the effects a writer or speaker hopes to achieve. Rhetoric and style involve questions of propriety: the use of language should be appropriate under the circumstances, and, as we have seen, meaning is often elusive, which complicates the idea of propriety. For example, how is Charles Spencer's (1997) eulogy at the funeral of his sister, Diana Spencer, Princess of Wales, appropriate?

> Diana was the very essence of compassion, of duty, of style, of beauty. All over the world she was a symbol of selfless humanity, a standard-bearer for the rights of the truly downtrodden, a truly British girl who transcended nationality, someone with a natural nobility who was classless, who proved in the last year that she needed no royal title to continue to generate her particular brand of magic.

Charles Spencer achieves clarity through his use of language appropriate for the occasion. Focusing on Diana's inherent qualities, or "essence," he uses the rhetorical schemes of anaphora (repeating the preposition "of" at the start of successive clauses) and asyndeton, omitting the conjunction *and* in his list of the qualities of her "essence" (before "of beauty"). The effect is to make her qualities seem timeless, a seemingly never-ending list of virtues entirely fitting, or appropriate, for the occasion.

Spencer then uses a series of free modifiers, adding on to the base clause "All over the world she was a symbol of selfless humanity." Each free modifier supplements our knowledge of her, building on that which precedes it and referring back to the base clause. The cumulative effect is impressive, with the final free modifier—"who proved in the last year that she needed no royal title to continue to generate her particular brand of magic"—adding to the climactic development of the sentence. Indeed, the scheme of climax, with each free modifier increasing in importance, is appropriate in enumerating the praise at a eulogy. Overall, the stylistic effect is to increase the clarity of the sentences, each element adding to and illuminating our understanding of her humanity.

An element of clarity involves considering what our audience needs from us at every moment they are reading what we have written. Even in a speech, with gestures and other facial and verbal clues, it is essential that the audience not feel lost. Thus it makes sense to anticipate the needs of readers or listeners— what they need at each step of the way as they are taking in various forms of discourse. How is it that writers are able to anticipate readers' needs?

It is often a tricky balancing act, requiring writers to decide how to combine content and style in a way that makes for effective communication and understanding. How much information is enough? How much is too much? If too much is provided, it can often be just as ineffective as too little. Readers will become overwhelmed by the details or will become bored by what they consider inessential minutiae. What, then, is the proper balance, and how do we find it? How does that balance affect clarity?

To help answer that question, consider the following excerpt from Andrew Holleran's (1988, 22) essay "Ground Zero," in which he describes the gradual change in New York City's response to the AIDS crisis as his friends were dying from the disease. While we cannot know all aspects of Holleran's thought process, we can analyze how he seems to make decisions about what to include, or exclude, from his account.

> Years ago, when the first friend died, those he'd left behind talked about his illness for months; the whole city seemed haunted by him; we could not imagine New York without Eddie.

In order to create a sense of suspense, Holleran begins with a periodic sentence in which the meaning is withheld until the end, building up from the start with "Years ago," "when the first friend died," and several successive clauses separated by semicolons that reinforce the importance of his friend, until the final word—when we discover his name, Eddie. The structure of the periodic sentence makes him the subject of interest throughout the city of New York—and larger than life. With each revelation, Holleran makes the reader want to know more and to read on until the revelation of Eddie's name.

As Holleran continues, he captures readers' interest by using details that allow us to imagine the exponential change in the status of the disease.

> Now when the news comes that the twenty-fifth or thirty-ninth friend has died, I discuss the death, and before hanging up the phone, ask the person who brings these tidings if he wants to go to the movies Tuesday. It's nearly banal. Won't someone please

turn off the bubble machine? We get the point. The friend who
lives upstate says calling friends in Manhattan is "like phoning
Germany in the thirties." Or, as a friend who lives in town puts it,
"It's like living in Beirut. You never know where the next bomb is
going to go off." The bomb seems the best metaphor as I wander
the Metropolitan. "Oh," people say when they learn someone left
New York in 1983, "you got out before the bomb fell." Well, not
really, he wants to reply, the bomb fell several years before that.
Only we didn't know it. The bomb fell without anyone's knowing
the bomb had fallen, which is how it destroyed a community that
now seems—looking back—as extinct as the Mayans.

When he writes that "now when the news comes that the
twenty-fifth or thirty-ninth friend has died," he asks readers to
see that the disease has become commonplace, "banal" in his
words. He then switches gears, capturing our attention by asking a rhetorical question—"Won't someone please turn off the
bubble machine?"—thus implying the need for the onslaught
of negative news to end. Having piqued our interest, he moves
into a set of similes, saying the AIDS plague is "like phoning
Germany in the thirties" and "like living in Beirut. You never
know where the next bomb is going to go off." The similes,
which make comparisons to horrific situations with which we
are familiar, make us want to know more.

In addition to the similes, Holleran also uses the metaphor of
AIDS as a bomb ("You never know when the next bomb is going
to go off"), but he does not stop simply with his use of the metaphor, instead complicating it by suggesting it was a stealth bomb
that devastated a community: "The bomb fell without anyone's
knowing." Claiming that AIDS "destroyed" the gay community,
Holleran again uses a simile, calling the community "as extinct
as the Mayans." The final simile offers readers a precise image
with which to end the passage, comparing the AIDS crisis to the
powerful idea of the extinction of the Mayan culture.

In each clause, then, Holleran creates the need, or desire, to
know more. He uses style, combined with content, to generate
curiosity in his readers, who find a reason, in every sentence—
and indeed in every clause—to keep going. The way we hang on
every word constitutes a form of clarity crucial to developing an
effective writing style.

■ Clarity and Transparent versus Opaque Style

There is a longtime debate in the field of rhetoric and composition and in related fields (literature, certainly) about the virtues of clarity. Richard Lanham (1983a, 58), a former professor at UCLA, has critiqued what he calls "C-B-S" style (clarity, brevity, sincerity). He says C-B-S style's language remains passive and transparent and urges writers to look *through* words to an underlying reality. He disagrees with that characterization. In contrast is an opaque style in which we look *at* the words themselves, characterized by reordering, exaggeration, discontinuity, and a return to play. He says, "Either we notice an opaque style as a style (i.e., we look at it) or we do not (i.e., we look through it to a fictive reality beyond)." Lanham is advocating a close look at the style to see what it yields and how it is being used to convey meaning. He suggests that what is on the surface is just as important as what lies below it.

■ Clarifying Your Style for Different Audiences

The idea of clarity varies according to the audience for which you might be writing. It is important to remember, though, that sometimes an audience finds it difficult to discern a clear meaning from an author's words. For instance, take this sentence by Rob Wilson (1994, 293) in "Cyborg America: Policing the Social Sublime in 'Robocop' and 'Robocop 2,'" part of an edited collection. Why do you think it won second place in the academic journal *Philosophy and Literature*'s annual Bad Writing Contest? Does the sentence seem clear to you?

> If such a sublime cyborg would insinuate the future as post-Fordist subject, his palpably masochistic locations as ecstatic agent of the sublime superstate need to be decoded as the "now-all-but-unreadable DNA" of a fast deindustrializing Detroit, just as his Robocop-like strategy of carceral negotiation and street control remains the tirelessly American one of inflicting regeneration through violence upon the racially heteroglossic wilds and others of the inner city.

Why does the sentence lack clarity? On the level of diction, several words, mostly adjectives or nouns, require specialized knowledge; those words include "post-Fordist," "superstate," "Robocop-like," "carceral," and "heteroglossic." While some of the words might be known to readers or understood from the context, their cumulative effect is to make the sentence virtually indecipherable to a number of readers.

The syntax also makes the sentence difficult to parse, especially given the abundance of adjectives that make it necessary to analyze expressions within every clause to achieve a full understanding. For example, we must wade through the adjectives "fast deindustrializing" to know how to understand Detroit; consider why the writer's strategy is both "Robocop-like" and "tirelessly American"; and contemplate what the "racially heteroglossic wilds" might look like. In short, the sentence's word order or arrangement makes it difficult to understand fully without stopping, and often rereading, individual clauses. Thus, the clarity of the sentence is sacrificed at every stage.

■ Clarity and Obfuscation

The NCTE Doublespeak Award, established in 1974 and given by the NCTE Public Language Award Committee, is an ironic tribute to public speakers who have perpetuated language considered "grossly deceptive, evasive, euphemistic, confusing, or self-centered." In 2016, NCTE awarded the Doublespeak Award to then-candidate Donald Trump. It acknowledges another lack of clarity often found in cultural, and political, settings. In its award, NCTE states,

> Trump repeatedly fails to communicate how the greater community would benefit from his proposals and instead often tends toward obfuscation and inconsistency. Many times he has made a statement one day and denied it in following days. Trump has the unique gift of capitalizing on what he labels the dishonesty of his opponent, all while spinning unsubstantiated claims of his own. In literary terms, Donald Trump might be viewed as an inconsistent or otherwise unreliable narrator. In rhetorical terms, he frequently honors pathos before logos, often speaking without substance and placing feelings above rationality. One committee member wrote, "I don't think we've ever had a better

example of the Doublespeak Award," and the five committee members unanimously voted Donald Trump as the champion of the dubious Doublespeak honor. (National Council of Teachers of English 2016)

■ How to Revise Writing for Clarity

How does something initially deemed unclear become clearer for readers? Different possibilities exist to help improve clarity. By considering the audience, it's possible to reduce some of the initial confusion through several techniques. One solution often cited by critics is to break long sentences up and achieve clarity by writing shorter sentences.

To help make sense of how to clarify writing, consider the following passage by Timothy W. Luke (1997, 15) from the article entitled "Museum Pieces: Politics and Knowledge at the American Museum of Natural History":

> Natural history museums, like the American Museum, constitute one decisive means for power to de-privatize and re-publicize, if only ever so slightly, the realms of death by putting dead remains into public service as social tokens of collective life, rereading dead fossils as chronicles of life's everlasting quest for survival, and canonizing now dead individuals as nomological emblems of still living collectives in Nature and History. An anatomo-politics of human and non-human bodies is sustained by accumulating and classifying such necroliths in the museum's observational/ expositional performances.

How can Luke's piece achieve greater clarity? Luke can simplify his sentences and eliminate academic jargon. The first sentence is especially inscrutable, as he seems to suggest that natural history museums have the power to make human and nonhuman remains of the dead more accessible by showing how dead fossils suggest the unending quest for survival and how dead humans are connected to living ones. In the second sentence, the word "necroliths" is relatively unknown and difficult to locate in a dictionary, just as "nomological" proves difficult in the first sentence. The use of obscure words hinders meaning and makes the text less accessible to many readers.

■ CONCISION

What makes writing concise? To answer that question, consider some examples above in this chapter of verbose writing in which too many words are used to convey a specific idea. Concision does not always mean writing with simple sentences, but sometimes using short sentences can be a mark of concision. The following paragraph from Ta-Nehisi Coates's (2015, 121) National Book Award-winning *Between the World and Me* is a good example:

> My ticket took me to Geneva first. Everything happened very fast. I had to change money. I needed to find a train from the airport into the city and after that find another train to Paris. Some months earlier, I had begun a halting study of the French language. Now I was in a storm of French, drenched really, and only equipped to catch drops of the language—"who," "euros," "you," "to the right." I was still very afraid.

In this instance, concision comes about at first because Coates does not use more than a minimum number of words to convey his ideas. The short, simple sentences that begin the paragraph gather a certain momentum, leading to a complex sentence about his "halting study of the French language" and another sentence in which he uses a metaphor—comparing learning French to a storm in which he is "drenched" in words and catches "drops" of language. His concision is buttressed in this sentence by his use of the scheme of parenthesis in which he interrupts the flow to indicate what these "drops" of language consist of: "—'who,' 'euros,' 'you,' 'to the right.'" Coates's use of asyndeton, the omission of *and* before "to the right," adds to the concise nature of his paragraph.

His final sentence, "I was still very afraid," lends symmetry to the paragraph, ending where it began, with a short, simple sentence. In this paragraph, concision exists at least in part in the rhythm, its simple sentences building to complex ones, the penultimate sentence serving as a kind of denouement before the final reconciliation in the final sentence, its brevity returning readers to a sense of normalcy.

■ Concision and Sentence Combining

Sentence combining has been around since the 1890s, but it was revived with the theoretical basis of generative-transformational grammar. It uses techniques of embedding, deletion, subordination, and coordination. It can lead to concision by combining sentences rather than forcing readers to read many short, simple sentences. While not as popular as it once was, sentence combining is still used productively today. Many writing teachers draw examples and exercises from sentence-combining texts. While designing exercises for specific rhetorical or classroom situations is often preferable, the amount of time required to design new exercises for each situation often favors drawing from well-established resources that have been developed over time.

Beginning in the 1960s, Donald Bateman and Frank Zidonis (1964) of Ohio State University conducted an experiment to determine whether teaching students transformational-generative grammar would reduce the incidence of errors in their writing. They found that students taught transformational-generative grammar made fewer errors and wrote more complex sentence structures. Afterward, Kellog Hunt (1965) tried to determine what the best measure of student maturity in writing was, and he found it is not sentence length, per se, but something he called a "minimal terminable" unit or a "T-unit." A T-unit, according to Hunt (1965, 20), is "a main clause with all of its appended modifiers, including subordinate clauses." A T-unit can be punctuated as a sentence would be; however, any sentence might contain more than one T-unit if it has more than one independent clause. Hunt found that the three best ways to indicate stylistic maturity were the average number of words per T-unit, the average number of clauses per T-unit, and the average number of words per clause. Later, Frank O'Hare (1973) was able to show that sentence combining without any grammar instruction at all could produce important gains in students' stylistic maturity.

There are two types of sentence-combining exercises, cued and open. Cued exercises have only one correct answer, and they suggest it by giving signals within or at the ends of certain kernel sentences. While sentence combining is ideal when designed for specific purposes, contexts, and audiences, some well-known volumes present excellent examples of the practice. Here are some samples from O'Hare's (1973, 86) NCTE research report on sentence combining. The first is a cued exercise drawn from exercises he used as part of his group experiment. It starts with instructions, followed by problems and answers.

Lesson Nineteen: Which/That, Who, and Whom

In this lesson we'll be practicing combining sentences with WHICH/THAT, WHO, and WHOM. For example, if you were given the following:

> Some of the engines were scheduled to be scrapped this year.
>
> The saboteurs have demolished the engines. (THAT)

you would write it like this:

> Some of the engines that the saboteurs have demolished were scheduled to be scrapped this year.

The explanation continues:

> Notice that engines, the repeated word, was replaced by that. You look for the repeated word when instructed to combine sentences with WHICH/THAT, WHO, and WHOM. Then you simply eliminate and substitute for one of the repeated words.
>
> You may be given the instruction (WHICH/THAT). This simply means that you can use either which or that. You pick the one you think sounds better. Remember also that (WHICH/THAT) can mean (JUST JOIN).
>
> A. In his letter Ralph enclosed a snapshot.
>
> > He had taken a snapshot during his visit with us. (WHICH/ THAT)
>
> B. In his letter Ralph enclosed a snapshot which he had taken during his visit with us.
>
> Or: In his letter Ralph enclosed a snapshot that he had taken during his visit with us.
>
> Or: In his letter Ralph enclosed a snapshot he had taken during his visit with us.

Another sentence-combining example:

A. Whenever our family dines at Dino's, Grandma insists on watching the chef.

The chef tosses the pizzas high into the air. (WHO)

B. Whenever our family dines at Dino's, Grandma insists on watching the chef who tosses the pizzas high into the air.

Here are some additional examples from O'Hare (1973, 90; 92):

A. The explorers saw formations.

The formations were *glistening*.

The formations were *black*.

The formations were *rock*.

The formations were *rising hundreds of feet into the air*.

The formations were *one of Asia's greatest wonders*.

B. The explorers saw glistening black rock formations rising hundreds of feet into the air, one of Asia's greatest wonders.

A. The seventh graders could not understand SOMETHING.

The seventh graders had worked hard on their assignments. (WHO)

The assignments were *English*.

They had worked *all year*.

Their teacher had assigned two reports for some reason. (WHY)

The reports were *written*.

The reports were *per week*.

The reports were *on some novels*.

The novels were *boring*.

The novels would make SOMETHING impossible. (WHICH/ THAT)

They would fully enjoy their summer vacations. (IT-FOR-TO)

B. The seventh graders who had worked hard on their English assignments all year could not understand why their teacher had assigned two written reports per week on some boring novels that would make it impossible for them to fully enjoy their summer vacations.

■ DIY

Try this sentence-combining exercise from Frank O'Hare's (1985, 73) *Sentencecraft: A Course in Sentence-Combining*:

The next letter comes from a viewer.

The viewer doesn't understand <u>something</u>. (WHO)

A polar bear would know <u>something somehow</u>. (HOW)

A polar bear is <u>living in the arctic region</u>. (WHERE)

<u>The sun never sets</u> in the arctic region. (WHERE)

The bear is <u>to go to sleep sometime</u>. (WHEN TO)

■ Open Exercises

Combine these sentences, part of open exercises, which do not include cues, from William Strong's (1994, 12) *Sentence-Combining: A Composing Book*.

The trout were blanketed.

The trout were called rainbows.

The blanketing was with ferns.

The ferns were green.

The ferns were sweet smelling.

10 | Cohesion, Coherence, and Emphasis

Even an ancient monster needs a name. To name an illness is
to describe a certain condition of suffering—a literary act before
it becomes a medical one. A patient, long before he becomes the
subject of medical scrutiny, visited the kingdom of the ill. To
relieve an illness, one must begin, then, by unburdening its story.

—SIDDHARTHA MUKHERJEE, *THE EMPEROR OF ALL
MALADIES: A BIOGRAPHY OF CANCER*

■ COHESION

Cohesion can be thought of as what makes the sentences or
sections of a paragraph, essay, or book work together, helping
achieve a degree of seamlessness that allows readers to readily
understand a writer's meaning. Cohesion often involves emphasis, the given-new contract, transitions, and other devices to help
achieve what is sometimes called a *sense of flow*. How does that
work in Siddhartha Mukherjee's (2010) Pulitzer Prize-winning
book, *The Emperor of All Maladies: A Biography of Cancer?*

■ Given and New Information

One guiding principle of cohesion is that readers can quickly
understand a writer's meaning when the writer starts sentences

DOI: 10.7330/9781607328100.c010

Sign representing the intersection of cohesion and coherence

with given, old, or known information before moving on to new information readers are seeing for the first time. Calling this the "given-new contract," Herbert H. Clark and Susan E. Haviland distinguish between two kinds of information in declarative sentences: "(1) information the speaker considers given—information he believes the listener already knows and accepts as true; and (2) information the speaker considers new—information he believes the listener does not yet know" (Clark and Haviland 1977, 3). They call it a "contract" since, in order to facilitate "reasonably efficient communication," the speaker and listener both give and interpret information in this way.

The idea is that readers are able to follow the flow of sentences more easily if they encounter given information—information familiar to them from what they have already read—before they confront new information. This follows what Clark and Haviland say is at the heart of the agreement: "It is a device that exists because the listener wants to integrate new information into what he already knows, and the device can work only because of an abstract agreement between speaker and listener, the given-new contract" (38).

For his part, Mukherjee begins by saying that an "ancient monster" needs a name, ending his sentence with the word "name." Notice that he begins the next sentence with "to name," the same word used first as a noun and then, in the second sentence, as a verb. The repetition of the same word helps readers recognize the word as old information that begins the second sentence before moving on to adding new information toward the end of that sentence. Similarly, the writer goes on to end his next sentence with the phrase "the kingdom of the ill" before beginning the following sentence with "To relieve an illness." Mukherjee changes the word slightly, using different forms of the same root word, "ill" and "illness," which are close enough to constitute the given-new contract (sometimes called the "known-new contract"), aiding the cohesiveness of the paragraph.

■ Cohesion at the Beginning and End of Sentences

Sometimes it is possible to achieve cohesion simply through the use of parallelism, or similarity in the structure of a series of words, phrases, or clauses used. Take, for instance, the following paragraph from Mukherjee's (2010, 46–47) *The Emperor of All Maladies*, which follows directly after the last example. Where does parallelism exist?

> The names of ancient illnesses are condensed stories in their own right. Typhus, a stormy disease, with erratic, vaporous fevers, arose from the Greek *tuphon*, the father of winds—a word that also gives rise to the modern *typhoon*. *Influenza* emerged from the Latin *influentia* because medieval doctors imagined that the cyclical epidemics of flu were influenced by stars and planets revolving toward and away from the earth. *Tuberculosis* coagulated out of the Latin *tuber*, referring to the swollen lumps of glands that looked like small *scrofula*, from the Latin word for "piglet," evoking the rather morbid image of a chain of swollen glands arranged in a line like a group of suckling pigs.

The paragraph achieves cohesion in part by the way it begins with two words—"names" and "stories"—used in the paragraph directly preceding it; thus, the words "names" and "stories," since they draw upon old information, make use of the given-and-new contract. Yet most of the cohesion occurs through Mukherjee's use of parallelism, his repetition of the same structure in a series. He achieves this by using nouns—specifically "typhus," "Influenza," and "Tuberculosis"—at the start of successive sentences to give readers placeholders and to order his paragraph cohesively.

If parallelism helps achieve cohesion at the beginning of sentences, what can help cohesiveness at the end of sentences? Consider how Scott Russell Sanders (1995, 734) achieves cohesion in two different ways, perhaps surprisingly through the use of the same pronoun. First, he achieves cohesion in a declarative sentence with a base clause and a series of free modifiers.

> Whatever my brother and sister and mother may be thinking
> on their own rumpled pillows, I lie there hating him, loving him,
> fearing him, knowing I have failed him.

In Sanders's sentence, he uses the same word ("him"), the repetition of the pronoun in successive clauses constituting the scheme of epistrophe as well as creating a sense of flow—emphasizing his father while at the same time distancing him through the pronoun "him." Sanders thus keeps him at arm's length, solidifying that sense of distance and solidarity by using polysyndeton, or the repetition of the same conjunction, marshaling the forces of "my brother *and* sister *and* mother" in opposition to "him," his father.

Notice how Sanders achieves a similar, but slightly changed, result with his use of interrogative sentences in the next passage. Throughout the passage, how does Sanders (1995, 739) achieve cohesion through the juxtaposition of parallelism at the end—as well as the beginning—of successive sentences?

> If my father was indeed possessed, who would exorcise him? If he
> was a sinner, who would save him? If he was ill, who would cure
> him? If he suffered, who would ease his pain? Not ministers or
> doctors, for we could not bring ourselves to confide in them; not
> the neighbors, for we pretended they had never seen him drunk;
> not Mother, who fussed and pleaded but could not budge him;
> not my brother and sister, who were only kids.

The repetition of "If my father was" or "If he was," an example of anaphora, sets up the question, "who would exorcise [or save or cure] him?," the latter an example of epistrophe. The two together, a scheme known as *symploce*, are repeated in the second part of the paragraph, with anaphora present in the word "not" and epistrophe with the word "for." The repeated use of symploce in Sanders's paragraph suggests the cohesive nature of parallelism. In this case, the paragraph represents unity, proportion, and balance as aspects of a cohesive style.

■ TAKE 2

Below is a paragraph that appears earlier in *TWS*. Notice its first use of the word "purpose" as new information before its repetition of "purpose" as known, or given, information, in subsequent sentences.

> Another part of using style in a specific context is our *purpose*.
> A *purpose* is always present behind our words, even if we are
> not fully aware of or able to articulate it. Some examples of that
> *purpose* are to amuse, to persuade, to inform, or to get someone's
> attention. Lincoln's *purpose* was arguably not only to honor the
> sacrifice of fallen soldiers but also to urge others to keep fighting
> to preserve the nation. Since our *purpose* is often inchoate,
> taking shape as we go along, we may not always anticipate, or
> intend, the results of our words.

The repetition of "purpose" creates cohesion since, after its first appearance, it becomes given information that helps readers see how the sentences are connected.

■ DIY

How does Peggy Orenstein (2010) achieve cohesion through parallelism in her *New York Times Magazine* article, "I Tweet, Therefore I Am"?

> When every thought is externalized, what becomes of insight?
> When we reflexively post each feeling, what becomes of reflec-
> tion? When friends become fans, what happens to intimacy?

■ Cohesion with the Passive Voice

While the passive voice has already been discussed in chapter 3, its use is reprised here as an aid to cohesion. How is it that the passive voice can facilitate or aid cohesion better than active verbs? To explain that, consider the following passage from Dee Brown's (1975, 8) acclaimed book *Bury My Heart at Wounded Knee*, also an Emmy award-winning film produced for television by HBO:

> In 1848 gold was discovered in California. Within a few months, fortune-seeking easterners by the thousands were crossing the Indian Territory. Indians who lived or hunted along the Santa Fe and Oregon trails had grown accustomed to seeing an occasional wagon train licensed for traders, trappers, or missionaries. Now suddenly the trails were filled with wagons, and the wagons were filled with white people. Most of them were bound for California gold, but some turned southwest for New Mexico or northwest for the Oregon country.

Notice that the use of the passive voice in such phrases as "gold was discovered in" and "the trails were filled with" helps make the passage cohesive. In the second sentence, by contrast, the *active* voice in the clause "thousands were crossing the Indian Territory" ends the sentence with "Indian Territory"—which is new information here—and the next sentence, which starts with "Indians," is now known or given information. It is useful to remember, then, that the known-new contract can be effectively used when sentences are in either the active or passive voice.

The next sentence, in fact, clearly benefits from the passive voice to achieve cohesion: "Now suddenly the trails were filled with wagons, and the wagons were filled with white people." The phrase "the trails" is known information, as it was introduced in the preceding sentence. By using the passive voice, "trails were filled with wagons," the clause ends with new information ("wagons") immediately picked up again as old information in the next clause ("and the wagons were filled with white people"), providing cohesion through the given-new contract. The clause "the wagons were filled with white people," also in the passive voice, sets up the next clause, "Most of them were bound." The pronoun "them" substitutes for "people," a use of the known-new contract.

Overall, then, Brown uses the passive voice in providing cohesive ties in his account of the way in which the California gold rush changed the western landscape with its huge influx of people into Indian Territory. The author creates a sense of clarity and flow with all the interconnecting ideas, joined together through the close juxtaposition of old, or given, and new information.

■ COHERENCE

While the terms *cohesion* and *coherence* are often used interchangeably, *TWS* makes an important distinction between them. Coherence refers to the way in which paragraphs and larger chunks of discourse make sense, that is, how readers are able to make sense of the whole. To that end, it involves the arrangement of sentences, paragraphs, essays, or chapters and how they fit together to help readers understand what is being written. *TWS* contends that coherence often fails when writers adopt a stance of what Linda Flower calls "writer-based prose," the antithesis of "reader-based prose."

According to Flower (1979, 37), writer-based prose is "a halfway place for many writers . . . a rich compilation of significant thoughts which cohere *for the writer* into a network she or he has not yet fully articulated." Writer-based prose is at the heart of writing readers might describe as "dense" or hard to decipher. Here are some of the characteristics Flower (1979, 19–20) identifies with writer-based prose:

> In *function*, Writer-Based prose is a verbal expression written by a writer to himself and for himself. It is the record and the working of his own verbal thought. In its *structure*, Writer-Based prose reflects the associative, narrative path of the writer's own confrontation with the subject. In its *language*, it reveals her use of privately loaded terms and shifting but unexpressed contexts for her statements.

Take, for instance, this sentence from Steven Z. Levine's (1996) article "Manet's Man Meets the Gleam of Her Gaze: A

Psychoanalytic Novel"—which appears in Bradford R. Collins's (1996) collection *Twelve Views of Manet's Bar*—in which the author, using writer-based prose, seems to fulfill all elements of Flower's writer-based prose. Notice how Levine thinks through his ideas without considering his audience. It was submitted as an entry in *Philosophy and Literature*'s Bad Writing Contest.

As my story is an august tale of fathers and sons, real and imagined, the biography here will fitfully attend to the putative traces in Manet's work of *les noms du père*, a Lacanian romance of the errant paternal phallus ("Les Non-dupes errant"), a revised Freudian novella of the inferential dynamic of paternity which annihilates (and hence enculturates) through the deferred introduction of the third term of insemination the phenomenologically irreducible dyad of the mother and child. (252–53)

As an alternative to writer-based prose lacking coherence, Flower (1979, 20) touts reader-based prose, which she defines as "a deliberate attempt to communicate something to a reader. To do that it creates a shared language and shared context between writer and reader." She goes on to compare writer- and reader-based prose, and, in the process, sheds light on the nature of coherence.

In its language and structure, Reader-Based prose reflects the *purpose* of the writer's thought; Writer-Based prose tends to reflect its *process*. Good writing, therefore, is often the cognitively demanding transformation of the natural but private expressions of Writer-Based thought into a structure and style adapted to a reader.

Many passages in *TWS* reflect reader-based prose that exemplifies coherence and a translation of private thoughts to public ones. A good book-length example can be found in Nobel Prize-winning Gabriel García Márquez's *News of a Kidnapping*. In the excerpt below, García Márquez (1997, 177), whose original Spanish version is translated by the renowned Edith Grossman, ends one chapter as follows:

The only certain road to freedom for the hostages led straight to the lion in his den. In plain language: The only thing left for him [Alberto Villamizar] to do—and he was bound to do it—was fly to Medellín and find Pablo Escobar, wherever he might be, and discuss the situation face-to-face.

Here is how García Márquez (1997, 178) opens the next chapter. Consider the ways in which the author makes the passage coherent for readers:

> The problem was how to find Pablo Escobar in a city martyrized by violence. In the first two months of 1991 there had been twelve hundred murders—twenty a day—and a massacre every four days. An agreement among almost all the armed groups had led to the bloodiest escalation of guerrilla violence in the history of the country, and Medellín was the center of urban terrorism. A total of 457 police had been killed in only a few months. The DAS had said that two thousand people in the slums were working for Escobar, many of them adolescents who earned their living hunting down police. For each dead officer they received five million pesos, for each agent a million and a half, and 800,000 for each one wounded. On February 16, 1991, three low-ranking officers and eight agents of the police were killed when a car was blown up with 150 kilos of dynamite outside the bullring in Medellín. Nine passersby were also killed and another 143, who had nothing to do with the war, were injured.

Readers are able to make sense of the paragraph because coherence comes initially from just a few keywords: "Pablo Escobar," "Medellín," and "violence," paired with other words like "urban terrorism." All of the sentences follow from these terms—already familiar to readers—and form part of the coherent whole. In addition, García Márquez achieves coherence by using vocabulary that coheres easily for readers. First, he uses a group of words associated with violence: "murder," "massacre," "hunting down," "dead," "wounded," "killed," "injured," "dynamite," and "war."

The author also makes the passage coherent by regularly inserting numbers that represent different types of statistics: the number of people killed ("twelve hundred" in two months or "twenty a day"; "a massacre every four days"); "457 police" officers; on a single day, "three low-ranking officers and eight [regular] agents," plus "nine passersby," with "143 . . . injured." The statistics also include the amount of money paid for human carnage—"For each dead officer they received five million pesos, for each agent a million and a half, and 800,000 for each one wounded"—and enumerate the "150 kilos" of dynamite used for a car bomb.

The consistency of vocabulary, statistics, and subject matter helps make García Márquez's writing coherent; even in translation, it is an outstanding example of reader-based prose, anticipating in many different ways how readers make sense of writing and furnishing many contextual clues along the way to help readers follow a roadmap to understanding.

■ DIY

What specific elements make the opening of chapter 4 in García Márquez's (1997, 69) *News of a Kidnapping* coherent?

> The abduction of journalists was, in effect, a response to the idea that had preoccupied President César Caviria since the time he was a minister in Virgilio Barco's government: how to create a judicial alternative to the war against terrorism. It had been a central theme in his campaign for the presidency. He had emphasized it in his acceptance speech, making the important distinction that terrorism by the drug traffickers was a national problem and might have a national solution, while the drug traffic was international and could only have international solutions. His first priority was narcoterrorism, for after the first bombs, public opinion demanded prison for the terrorists, after the next few bombings the demand was for extradition, but as the bombs continued to explode public opinion began to demand amnesty. For this reason, extradition had to be considered an emergency measure that would pressure the criminals into surrendering, and Gaviria was prepared to apply that pressure without hesitation.

■ EMPHASIS

It probably goes without saying that the natural emphasis falls at the end, rather than at the beginning, of most sentences. Whether because the form of a sentence creates an expectation for a resolution, or because we simply look to endings for the completion of ideas, we are often able to anticipate where the emphasis falls. Consider, for instance, the following paragraph from Ta-Nahisi Coates's (2015, 129) *Between the World and Me*, and see where the emphasis falls in each sentence:

> I did not die in my aimless youth. I did not perish in the agony of not knowing. I was not jailed. I had proven to myself that there was another way beyond the schools and the streets. I felt myself to be among the survivors of some great natural disaster, some plague, some avalanche or earthquake. And now, living in the wake of a decimation and having arrived at a land that I once considered mythical, everything seemed cast in a halo—the pastel Parisian scarves burned brighter, the morning odor wafting out of the boulangeries was hypnotic, and the language all around me struck me not so much as language but as dance.

Coates's first three sentences are loose, meaning we understand almost at the start that the author (1) did not die, (2) did not perish, and (3) was not jailed. In all three sentences, however, the real meaning—the heart—of the sentence comes at the end. At the end of the sentences, we learn the crucial context that forms the beginning of his sentences. The three sentences also lead to his important fourth sentence, where, once again, the emphasis comes at the end:

> I had proven to myself that there was another way beyond the schools and the streets.

In this sentence, the emphasis leads to the end, where we understand that he discovers there is a world beyond the narrow one in which he grew up.

The rest of the paragraph also reveals the importance of placing emphasis at the end of sentences. When he writes "I felt myself to be among the survivors of some great natural disaster, some plague, some avalanche or earthquake," he uses the scheme of climax, in which each phrase—"some great natural disaster, some plague, some avalanche or earthquake"—increases in importance, with the final phrase adding specificity to the significant nature (like an avalanche or earthquake) of his survival.

Similarly, with the final loose, or cumulative, sentence, which begins with Coates's base clause "And now, living in the wake of a decimation and having arrived at a land that I once considered mythical, everything seemed cast in a halo," readers understand the author's meaning immediately, and, indeed, the sentence could end there. However, Coates is not finished: he uses the scheme of parenthesis, a sudden interruption (signaled by a dash), which sends the sentence in another direction—away from "the wake of decimation" and into the land of the mythical.

> —the pastel Parisian scarves burned brighter, the morning odor
> wafting out of the boulangeries was hypnotic, and the language
> all around me struck me not so much as language but as dance.

■ CRITICAL THINKING

1. What makes the following sentences cohesive? They are from Nick Carr's (2008) "Is Google Making Us Stupid?"

> Over the past few years I've had an uncomfortable sense
> that someone, or something, has been tinkering with my
> brain, remapping the neural circuitry, reprogramming the
> memory. My mind isn't going—so far as I can tell—but
> it's changing. I'm not thinking the way I used to think. I
> can feel it most strongly when I'm reading. Immersing
> myself in a book or a lengthy article used to be easy. My
> mind would get caught up in the narrative or the turns
> of the argument, and I'd spend hours strolling through
> long stretches of prose. That's rarely the case anymore.
> Now my concentration often starts to drift after two or
> three pages. I get fidgety, lose the thread, begin looking for
> something else to do.

2. Where does the emphasis fall in the following excerpt from Sherry Turkle's (2012, 11) *Alone Together: Why We Expect More from Technology and Less from Each Other*?

> As we instant-message, e-mail, text and Twitter, tech-
> nology redraws the boundaries between intimacy and
> solitude. We talk of getting "rid" of our e-mails, as though
> these notes are so much excess baggage. Teenagers
> avoid making telephone calls, fearful that they "reveal
> too much." They would rather text than talk. Adults, too,

choose keyboards over the human voice. It is more efficient they say. Things that happen in "real time" take too much time. Tethered to technology, we are shaken when that world "unplugged" does not signify, does not satisfy. After an evening of avatar-to-avatar talk in a networked game, we feel at one moment in possession of a full social life and in the next curiously isolated, in tenuous complicity with strangers. We build a following on Facebook or MySpace and wonder to what degree our followers are friends. We recreate ourselves as online personae and give ourselves new bodies, homes, jobs and romances. Yet, suddenly, in the half-light of virtual community, we may feel utterly alone. As we distribute ourselves, we may abandon ourselves. Sometimes people experience no sense of having communicated after hours of connection. And they report feelings of closeness when they are paying little attention. In all of this, there is a nagging question: Does virtual intimacy degrade our experience of the other kind and, indeed, of all encounters of any kind?

11 | Practicing Style

Many of us are not used to thinking about how language works to produce specific effects. That's one of the biggest challenges in learning about style. In addition, like rhetoric, style sometimes has unpopular cultural associations that can make us skeptical in approaching the topic. Some resist the premise that language can (or should) be used to elicit certain responses from readers or listeners and do not trust the idea of studying rhetorical effects. What's more, many people have never been introduced to style as a way of studying language as a mode of analysis.

The assignments that follow are designed to help cultivate the ability to develop the use of style in writing. They are presented together here but are available to readers and writers after finishing chapters in *The Writer's Style*. It might be helpful to know the learning objectives that form the basis of assignments. They are to help you (1) understand some of the history and meaning of style; (2) develop reading and writing strategies, including knowledge of stylistic choices; (3) acquire stylistic knowledge and control of your own writing style; (4) learn how to use style in specific rhetorical situations, including in a projected career or profession; (5) develop proficiency in revision (including, but not limited to, editing); (6) deepen your love for the English language, its potential and promise.

DOI: 10.7330/9781607328100.c011

Representation of style using an allusion to "Got Milk?" campaign

▪ ASSIGNMENT 1: ANALYSIS OF DIDION'S STYLE

For the first essay, analyze Joan Didion's (1961) style in her well-known piece, "Goodbye to All That." This assignment introduces several methods of stylistic analysis to help you see the ways in which style can be valuable as critical thinking. The essay prompt below should help you to understand how style and content work together to produce meaning:

> Analyze Joan Didion's style in her essay "Goodbye to All That"
> and discuss how the author uses stylistic resources to achieve
> certain effects. Use what we have learned to complete the analy-
> sis. In other words, you may want to look at the author's use
> of level(s) of style ("high," "middle," "low," or a combination) or
> diction (formal versus informal or colloquial), voice, vocabulary/
> word choice, usage, syntax (including her use of free modifiers
> and left-, right-, and midbranching sentences), as well as her use
> of tropes and schemes. It will be useful to think about Didion's
> use of the three rhetorical appeals (logos, pathos, ethos) and how
> each helps her achieve her purpose in this particular rhetorical
> situation. Don't be afraid to describe a rhetorical or stylistic tech-
> nique used by Didion even if you don't know its technical name.
> In other words, your analysis of her style is more important
> than your identification of a precise rhetorical or stylistic term.

You are encouraged to choose a central theme, thesis, claim, or argument to guide your essay. For example, you could discuss the way Didion uses antithesis to frame the two opposing ways she sees New York City. You might argue that the two oppositions result in a coherent whole—or that they are fragmentary, representing the way an individual is often conflicted in our postmodern culture.

It can be difficult to immediately make claims about the rhetorical counterforces at work in Didion's essay. Thus, it's helpful to discuss potential claims about what Didion's style reveals—possible arguments for the essay. Here are a few examples of working claims from past discussions:

- While Didion's "Goodbye to All That" seems at first a nostalgic attempt to recover the lost innocence of her youthful experiences in New York City, the essay's style actually reflects a writer coming to terms with the realities of her failed experiment read, as it were, through the lens of the Big Apple's antithesis, Los Angeles.

- Even though Joan Didion's "Goodbye to All That" appears to extol the virtues of New York City in a forward-looking elegy to youth, newness, and optimism, its antithetical structure and style betray the author's true viewpoint: a nightmarish retrospection on the decline and deterioration of aging in an unforgiving city.

- Although the images of light and life in Joan Didion's "Goodbye to All That" may depict what seems to be an emotionally balanced view of New York City, the essay's diction, syntax, and figures of speech suggest just the opposite—the ultimate triumph of depression over hope as the author slips, perhaps unwittingly, into a world of darkness, lethargy, and despair.

Notice that the ideas themselves are fairly narrow; however, the stylistic methods Didion uses are stated in fairly broad terms in the thesis statement. Why is that? You will have a lot of details to add about how Didion uses style to achieve effects in her essay. For that reason, in the claim or argument (thesis statement), it makes sense to mention the stylistic resources in general terms. For instance, you can elaborate on her use of syntax (word arrangement), diction (choice of words), sentence variation, figures of speech, levels of style, periodic versus loose or running sentences, and more in the body of the essay itself.

It's also useful to examine some specific examples of how you might analyze Didion's diction: if, for example, you see the essay as more negative or dark, you might look for words that convey or depict a darker or more depressive state of mind. A few possibilities include "not," "irrevocable" (at least in the way she uses it), "mistake," and perhaps even her use of "love" (which doesn't seem overly optimistic in her essay). You might also look at the way many of her words seem to be abstract or distant: for instance, her use of metonymy ("Wall Street," "Fifth Avenue," "Madison Avenue"), in which she seems not to have any personal connection with the names used to describe activities that go on there (finance, fashion, advertising). Note, too, her use of synecdoche ("faces"), in which the part stands for the whole, the often inscrutable faces of those Didion meets standing for the entire person (and possibly for their personas as well).

In looking at the antithetical structure of Didion's essay, it's possible to examine, in addition to the scheme of antithesis itself, the difference in her use of asyndeton and polysyndeton; anaphora and epistrophe; ellipsis and amplification (the long sentences she adds after introducing an idea); and the variation in her use of long and short sentences. Feel free to add to all these ideas and investigate the ways in which antithesis plays an important role in the essay, at times working against the author's apparent intent.

In preparing to write the essay, the most important thing you can do is to try to *see* something. In other words, what do *you* think is really going on in this essay? What do you think the essay is about? I urge you not to worry about what others have said about Didion's essay but to come up with your own idea and then look for evidence of how Didion demonstrates that idea stylistically, whether she intends to do so or not. Remember that writers can use style consciously or unconsciously.

Be sure to identify schemes and tropes in Didion's essay. By picking out various rhetorical figures of speech in "Goodbye to All That," you can do a close reading of Didion's essay while focusing on the author's possible meanings.

■ ASSIGNMENT 2: STYLISTIC ANALYSIS OF YOUR OWN PROSE

Analyze an essay you have written for another class to learn more about who you are as a writer. Given the work we have already studied in the class, you'll have a wide array of resources from which to draw in writing this essay. Here is a general list of some of the ways to analyze your own writing style.

■ Sentence-Level Concerns

Diction: general or specific; abstract or concrete; formal or informal; common words or jargon; denotative (referential) or connotative (emotive)

Length of sentences

Kinds of sentences: simple, compound, complex; compound-complex; cumulative ("loose"), periodic, balanced, antithetical; statement, question, command, exclamation

■ Figures of Speech: Schemes and Tropes

You may be surprised to learn that you use many stylistic techniques in your writing and that you tend to include figures of speech. A few common schemes are parallelism, anaphora, asyndeton, ellipsis, and apposition. You'll also find that you use similes and metaphors and occasionally rhetorical questions or even synecdoche or metonymy. It can be helpful to look at schemes and tropes grouped in various categories (see Corbett and Connors 1999):

- *Schemes of Parallelism*: parallelism, isocolon, antithesis
- *Schemes of Reversal*: anastrophe, chiasmus, antimetabole
- *Schemes of Repetition*: alliteration, assonance; anaphora, epistrophe, epanalepsis, anadiplosis, antimetabole, polyptoton
- *Schemes of Addition or Omission*: asyndeton, polysyndeton, ellipsis, parenthesis
- *Schemes of Arrangement*: climax, parenthesis
- *Tropes*: metaphor, simile, synecdoche, periphrasis, personification, hyperbole, litotes, rhetorical question, irony, onomatopoeia, paradox

■ **Cohesive Devices: Transitions; Known-New Contract; Metadiscourse**

Sometimes, after studying style, you may realize your writing would benefit from stylistic techniques like the given-and-new contract, in which one begins sentences with known or given information and ends them with new information to improve cohesion. Similarly, you might recognize that you use metadiscourse in ways that are not always helpful—especially the use of hedges (e.g., *sometimes, perhaps, might*) and intensifiers (e.g., *obviously, always, proves*) in ways that may affect your credibility as writers. Analyzing your own prose often means you learn to see how to use connotation and denotation to achieve different effects.

Next, complete a statistical analysis of your words using an activity developed by Edward P. J. Corbett and Robert J. Connors (1999). To complete the analysis, calculate the total number of words in the essay you're analyzing; the total number of sentences; the longest, shortest, and average sentences (in number of words); the number of sentences that contain more than ten words *over* the average sentence as well as the percentage of sentences that contain more than ten words over the average; the number of sentences that contain five words or more *below* the average and the percentage of sentences that contain five words or more below the average; the paragraph length, with the longest paragraph, shortest, and average paragraph (measured in the number of sentences). For the sake of comparison, compare your totals with that of a professional writer, F. L. Lucas, cited in the Corbett and Connors (1999) text. The comparison will give you a kind of average by which to measure your own writing.

Another helpful way to analyze your prose comes courtesy of Richard Lanham (2007, x) and his "paramedic method" for uncovering verbosity in language, what Lanham calls "lard." The goal is to help you improve concision. You'll find it useful in helping identify the overuse of prepositions, the use of *to be* verbs rather than active verbs, and the passive voice. You'll also learn when you have adopted a nominal, or noun, style of writing, especially when that comes at the expense of a style normally using active verbs. It's also helpful to examine your use of periodic versus cumulative (or "loose") sentences.

Finally, look at where your essay falls on the spectrum of correctness, clarity, emphasis, cohesion, and coherence, concepts we have studied throughout the semester. You may be surprised to learn about your stylistic strengths, and you will also discover some possibly unexpected things about your weaknesses or areas for improvement. Try to analyze how you tend to use style in your writing, and be open to learning how to incorporate stylistic techniques in future writing projects.

■ ASSIGNMENT 3: WRITING IN YOUR OWN STYLE

In this assignment, use style to achieve some of your writing goals. There are many options for you to choose what to write about (see below for a few ideas). In addition to the essay itself, write a two-page memo to explain what stylistic techniques you incorporated, how those techniques worked, and how knowing about the elements of style helped you in the writing process. I encourage you *not* to think about style explicitly as you are writing your essay. While you may decide to incorporate stylistic elements after the fact, the goal is to simply become aware of what features appear regularly in your writing.

The following list of elements for writing successful essays is relevant because you have the option of writing several types of essays, including those belonging to the genre of creative nonfiction.

- Show, don't tell, by using words to convey the image that will let the reader experience the point, not just hear what it is. Write for the effects the words have on a reader rather than to convey information.
- Use senses, especially those other than seeing.
- Start *in medias res*.
- Use flashback (or flashforward).
- Build suspense—try using a surprise ending.
- Use humor.
- Try an unusual point of view.
- Rearrange scenes or paragraphs.
- Cut the fat.
- Use allusions to nonfiction (or literary) texts, characters, or events.

- Be conscious of pacing.: is the tempo and rhythm of the text established in the first page or so and consistently continued to the end?

Here are some sample topics I hope you will consider as heuristics for this essay assignment. They are offered as aids to invention as you decide which topics to write about. Feel free to combine topics, to take them in a new or different direction, or simply to use them as the basis for discovering your own ideas—by far the most desirable outcome. Here are some general topics about place, travel, time, adventure, and identity to help you get started.

Place or Travel: Write about a place that holds special significance for you. Describe it in detail, but keep in mind that description has a purpose: to convey something larger about the feeling or meaning of the place. How does the patina of time and memory change or transform that place for you?

Picture a Place: Begin with the description of a photograph and let that photograph frame the topic of your essay. How does the photo, in itself, tell a story or feature aspects of the story that may have seemed to be in the background before?

Remembrance of Things Past: In a book by the same title, Marcel Proust writes about the effect of a *madeleine,* a small French pastry that, in combination with the taste and smell of tea, unleashes a host of memories and emotions. Write about your own Proustian experience, a time when a smell, taste, or another sense unlocked (or unleashed) a host of uncontrollable memories, thoughts, and/or feelings.

City of Dreams: Have you ever visited another city for the first time and asked yourself, "Where have you been all of my life?" Write about a city that holds special significance for you. What is it about the city that resonates with you? What is it that makes the city attractive in your eyes? Describe places, people, sights, sounds, smells.

Road Trip: Have you taken a trip across the country (or in a foreign country) that has changed your outlook or attitudes? Where did you go, what did you see, and what makes this more than the standard road trip? You might consider the road trips made famous by Hunter S. Thompson, Jack Ker-ouac, and others. Consider an eclectic (dysfunctional) family that travels across country, and see if that fits your personal circumstances.

Into the Wild: Have you ever had the kind of experience Jon Krakauer chronicles in his book (and in the movie) *Into the Wild*? If so, write about your adventure. What prompted your solo journey? What were you seeking? What did you find? Why was your outcome so different from Chris McCandless's in Krakauer's book?

Journey of Hope: Choose something in your life that moved from an overwhelmingly negative experience to a positive one and show how you were transformed from despair to hope. This involves, at a fundamental level, a personal journey, inner growth that has changed your life.

Across Five Aprils: Trace the development of something over a period of time—months or years—revisiting it each time from a slightly different perspective. The key here is to choose a fairly specific event, seen differently each time as you grow, change, and become a different person.

Identity Crisis: Describe a struggle with identity you've had growing up. There are traditional struggles—race, class, gen-der, ethnicity, religion, sexual orientation, community—but also less easily classified ones: student-scholar versus non-student, extrovert (social) versus introvert (loner), musician, writer, athlete, leader. Focus on the conflict between the you others want you to be and the one you wish to become.

A Deal with Dr. Faustus: Write about a time you compromised about something and it turned out to be a bad decision. Why did you make this "deal with the devil"?

Failure to Success/Victim to Survivor/Danger to Safety: Write about how someone you know turned their life around after facing uncommon odds.

Explanation or How-To: Choose something you are interested in or that you can write about particularly well from your own perspective. For instance, an essay about how to navigate the job search might be fascinating. But try to take a different angle on it. Most people probably think simply in terms of finding a good job. But how do you think about the job as part of your overall goals, life plans, lifestyle, and desires? Consider these possible topics.

How to Navigate Your City: How can others find the unknown places that make your city "the most livable city"?

How to Choose the Right Graduate Program: Law school? Master's in English? MBA? What's right for you and how do you think critically about that choice?

How to Reach Students Effectively: A guide for professors about what students really want (and need) from them in college. (Yes, I would love to read this article!)

How to Fill the Blank Page: Tips for invention or starting to write when you're drawing a blank and facing an empty screen. Share the collective wisdom you have amassed about writing.

Writing about Science or Nature: Your essay should fit the topic of science and nature writing. Think broadly and creatively about possible options. Don't be afraid to try something new, but choose a topic you are passionate about. A few possibilities follow.

Aurora Borealis: Write about a natural phenomenon you have experienced in your lifetime: the Northern Lights, a volcano, natural hot springs, whale watch, and so forth. Use observation and sensory details to explore how nature creates an awe-inspiring phenomenon or, to use Keats's phrase, "A thing of beauty is a joy forever."

Medical Miracle/Debacle: Describe a personal experience (involving you either directly or tangentially) that shows a struggle with modern medicine, its hopes and disappointments. Use narrative techniques to help make the essay come alive.

Science Demystified: Write about a popular scientific concept most people take for granted but don't know much about, and give it a new life by explaining it for a general, popular audience. Don't be afraid to use metaphors and other stylistic techniques to make the writing vivid and powerful.

Walden Pond Reclaimed: Write about your own Henry David Thoreau/Annie Dillard-type experience in which you explore a natural setting and investigate the interactions between human and natural contexts or occasions.

People's Best Friend(s): Describe or explain the relationship between you and your pet(s). What can that relationship teach us about life, nature, health, happiness, science, and our relationships with people we don't already know?

Essay from an Unusual Perspective: Ground your essay with an unusual point of view, perspective, subject matter, tense, time, or season. Turn the banal into the sublime; make your prose sing; find a metaphor that unifies your essay or makes it wince. Look for the eccentric within quotidian experiences. Focus on language, its multiple possibilities, its beauties, its limitations. Write from the heart: find something you care about and let it rise organically from the detritus of your past experience, your pain, your passion, your equivocation, your uncertainty. Let the form fit the content; don't be afraid to experiment. However, don't forsake clarity for novelty. Remember that readers must be drawn to your writing; don't expect it to be love at first sight. A few examples follow.

Urban Renewal: Write how a space surrounded by tall skyscrapers (office buildings) and concrete becomes transformed through plants, flowers, and imagination. Consider the anomaly, a deviation from the norm. How did you (or someone else) transform the space and create a new form of urban renewal?

Imagine a Great University: Conventional wisdom suggests a university's ascent to Tier One status results from a robust research agenda, national and international grants, and new buildings and programs, among other things. Write about what *you* think constitutes a great university. What is required for a university to truly rise to new heights?

Commencement Address: Commencement addresses are often widely read, and they are frequently quoted as among some of the most memorable writing of all time. Unfortunately, relatively few individuals are asked to give commencement addresses. Take this opportunity to write a commencement address for a group of students, parents, college professors, university officials, and others in attendance. Choose your own university, a college you attended in the past, or one you admire or aspire to attend. Read some famous commencement speeches to get a sense of the genre before you write.

Finding Your Bliss: Write about work you are pursuing or want to pursue as a passion. What makes you excited enough to wake up every day and want to do that work? What makes it seem like a job you would do even if you weren't paid? How did you find your bliss? What about it keeps you going and gives your life meaning?

Zen Garden: In our increasingly hectic lives, when many people are on the go most of the time, where do we turn for peace, tranquility, recuperation? What restores a sense of balance in our lives? Choose chapels, yoga, meditation, running, or something else. Write about an unusual way you (or others) found to reestablish your equilibrium.

Random Acts of Kindness: It has become a cliché of sorts that as a culture we are consumed with getting ahead, with our own well-being, and with a let-them-eat-cake mentality. Going against conventional wisdom, write about why kindness toward others is important in our culture. What do we get from it? How do we benefit as a society? Why should there be a prevailing attitude of kindness, as opposed to solipsism?

"I'm Going Nucking Futs": The anagram from the 1970s is suggestive of a bygone era that brought us disco, bell bottoms, and a continuation of flower power, hippies, and antiwar sentiment. Why should we look back at the 1970s, 1980s, 1990s, 2000s, and/or the 2010s as more than nostalgic constructions? Are there ideas, cultural trends, fashions, movements, or technologies that should be reconsidered, resurrected, or rethought in 2020? What can we (re)learn from the past?

Time Management: Are you able to plan time effectively or are you the type of person who lives from crisis to crisis? With everyone suffering from a time deficit, write about techniques to balance our personal and professional lives. How can we have time to fit in everything important to us in our lives? What does work-life balance mean today?

The Tipping Point: Choose a cultural trend you feel has reached a tipping point. What has made this particular thing, idea, or phenomenon tip at this particular time in our culture, or why do you think it will tip in a certain way in the future?

Willing Suspension of Disbelief: We once agreed to willingly suspend our disbelief to see into the lives of fictional characters. Why do we now want to pierce the veil of everyday lives as we do, for instance, on reality television? Why are ordinary people celebrated for rude behavior, talent (or lack of talent), or hard-luck stories? Where is this trend leading us as a culture?

Essay on a Pivotal Experience That Shaped or Changed Your Life: Write about an aspect of your past in which you have followed your dreams, overcome hardship, or discovered an unknown (but natural) affinity for something that changed your life. The point is to (re)examine an aspect of your life that was pivotal in some way in shaping the person you are today. The essay might focus on a special talent (e.g., music, singing, or acting), a subject area (e.g., science or math) you find easy and fun, a goal (practical or not) you set for yourself to reach, a hardship you faced but overcame.

■ ASSIGNMENT 4: THE WRITING STYLE IN A FUTURE DISCIPLINE, PROFESSION, OR CAREER

This assignment asks you to analyze the writing style in a discipline, profession, or career you hope to enter. The assignment consists of two parts: (1) writing an analytical essay discussing the specific writing style used in the discipline you choose and (2) delivering a ten-minute presentation in front of the class to discuss your analysis in the essay.

Be sure to draw on all the stylistic resources we have used all semester. While there are many possibilities, focus on some areas we have studied related to style directly or to those connected to rhetoric and the rhetorical situation in important ways.

Genre: What aspects of the author's writing have to do with genre or the form of writing (e.g., an essay, report, advertisement, legal brief, etc.)? What aspects of the writing form a part of the discourse (language in action) of this profession? In other words, how do you know the author is writing a specific form of discourse? What does the genre say about writing in this profession?

Oral Traditions and Voice: What elements of a traditional oral style exist in the writing? What about the rhythms of the writing and the way it reflects an authorial voice? How is the voice distinctive, and why does that make sense for the profession you might enter in the future?

Register or Levels of Style: Does the author use "high," "middle," or "low" style, or is there a mixture of levels of style? Does the author translate from "high" to "low" style? How is the level of style appropriate for the discourse community you hope to enter?

Allusions: What can you discern about the writing from the allusions (references to other authors, books, ideas, etc.) the author makes? Whom does the author refer to? Who are they? For what purpose are they citing these individuals, cases, references, and so forth?

Purpose: What is the purpose of this article? Is the author trying to persuade, entertain, instruct, or inform? How can you tell what the purpose is? Is the language denotative or connotative? What about the use of adjectives? Is the writer trying to accomplish something with specific adjectives or other uses of style?

Audience: How would you describe the audience? What knowledge is the audience assumed to have? What is the educational level of most readers, and how is it possible to discern that information from the author's style? What values or attitudes does the author assume on the part of readers? How does the author's implied audience give us clues into the profession itself?

Form: What do you notice about the form of the writing? How is it structured? Are paragraphs short or long (or both)? Are there any drawings or images? How does the writer tie form to the writing? What does the form say about the type of writing done in this profession? Does it create an expectation for completion?

Syntax: What do you notice about the structure of the author's sentences? Are they short or long? Simple, compound, complex, compound-complex? How does the writer arrange sentences? (Where are the most important ideas found? What does this say about the writer's emphasis?) Do they use parallelism? Loose or periodic sentences? Free modifiers? Left-, mid-, or right-branching sentences? Hypotactic or paratactic sentences?

Diction: What words or phrases reflect the writer's membership in this profession? What words are colloquial or jargon? Does the author repeat words or deliberately vary choices? What is unusual (if anything) about the author's vocabulary? What do the writer's diction and vocabulary say about the career/profession you hope to enter and the characteristics of writing in it?

Figures of Speech: What schemes and tropes does the author use? Why do they seem appropriate for this type of writing? What do they say about the profession or writing in it? Be sure to examine, and draw from, schemes of parallelism (parallelism, isocolon, tricolon, antithesis); of reversal (anastrophe, chiasmus, antimetabole); of repetition (alliteration; assonance, anaphora, epistrophe, epanalepsis, anadiplosis, antimetabole, polyptoton); of addition or omission (asyndeton, polysyndeton, ellipsis, parenthesis); of arrangement (climax, parenthesis); and such tropes as irony, metaphor, simile, metonymy, synecdoche, rhetorical question, hyperbole, litotes, onomatopoeia, and paradox.

Cohesive Devices and Use of Metadiscourse: How are transitions, cohesive devices, and other forms of metadiscourse used in the writing of this discipline? Why does it seem important? Does the discipline use hedges? Consider known-new contract (cohesion); emphasis (new information at the end); here, what-shifts, it-shifts, not only but also; conciseness.

The "Paramedic" Method: What does the use of *to be* verbs and of prepositional phrases say about this particular discipline? How prevalent is the use of the passive voice?

Tone: How does the author use tone (e.g., irony) in their writing and what can you infer about writing in this profession from the nature of that tone?

■ HARPER'S INDEX ESSAY ASSIGNMENT

In a group, prepare your own version of the *Harper's* Index using ideas and resources you collect together. Each group is responsible for researching, writing, editing, and preparing a list of Works Cited for the project. There is latitude in how you prepare your version of the index, but be sure to draw from some of the trends apparent in the index. Keep in mind there are certain conventions that adhere to the genre. The *Harper's* Index relies heavily on juxtaposition, the rhetorical situation (purpose, audience, and exigency), some audience knowledge or familiarity with the topic, and the use of certain rhetorical schemes and tropes, especially ellipsis, but also alliteration, assonance, anaphora, metaphor, and irony, among others. *Harper's* editor Lewis Lapham called the index a "single page of numbers that measure, one way or another, the drifting tide of events" (quoted in Brueggemann 1990, 220).

Here are some of the required components of the project.

- *Harper's* Index: As a group, complete a one-page index, roughly equivalent to the *Harper's* Index in *Harper's Magazine*.
- List of Works Cited: Cite your sources, including electronic sources, using MLA format.
- Reflection: Write individual two-page reflections about the process of writing the group's *Harper's* Index. How did you generate ideas? How did the process of collaboration work? What effect did the project have on you as a writer? What did you learn from writing in this genre? For example, what about the concise format? The use of juxtaposition and ellipsis? What can you apply to your writing in the future, and why?

These assignments are an excellent introduction to the study of style. You will be able to focus on a canon of rhetoric long ignored in classroom settings. In the end, you'll be able to develop an area of expertise to use in future courses as well as in your professional lives. You will develop a form of expertise others only rarely discuss in classes or outside the classroom setting. Learning about style will make a difference for you and will help you learn about varied aspects of writing and rhetorical study.

12 Epilogue

In this chapter, I respond to a prompt from chapter 11, "Practicing Style," drawn from the Place or Travel category. The brief essay, "Le Croissant d'Or," was written without conscious regard for stylistic techniques, which is probably true for most writers when they set about drafting something for the first time. Now that I have written extensively about stylistic resources in *The Writer's Style*, I thought it would be appropriate to reconsider this short work in the context of style. I have analyzed the essay's style, revising it deliberately, and, perhaps, even artistically, by drawing from techniques discussed in *TWS*.

In light of all of the chapters about style in *TWS*, I decided to follow up the essay by writing a short reflection on how different stylistic devices work in the brief narrative. I then think about how conscious knowledge of style now allows me to make changes to strengthen the essay. The proposed revisions draw on some of the stylistic techniques discussed in *The Writer's Style* and offer alternative approaches specifically informed by the study of style.

◼ LE CROISSANT D'OR

When you walk through the doors of Le Croissant d'Or Patisserie in the French Quarter of New Orleans, you feel you've stepped

DOI: 10.7330/9781607328100.c012

Le Croissant d'Or Patisserie in New Orleans

into a café off the Champs-Élysées. The smell of freshly baked baguettes and just-brewed café au lait invites you to linger at this eatery on Ursulines Avenue, just blocks from Bourbon Street and Jackson Square.

The dim winter sun filters through clear glass windows on a Sunday afternoon, dividing the room in half, part in the shadows. Sixteen round tables, all white, are positioned casually around the restaurant, surrounded by chairs with wire backs that curve up into a heart shape. At a table in the sunlight a man sits with his two young sons. He speaks with an accent, possibly Greek; his sons are speaking English without a trace of accent.

A few tables away, a man sits alone, drinking coffee. He gets up, goes to a black bin filled with newspapers, and leafs carelessly through the stack, returning to his table with Sunday's edition of the *Times-Picayune*. In his late thirties, maybe forty, he looks across to another café patron: a tall young man, in his mid- to late twenties, who is reading a book in the shadows. The young man, a red scarf around his neck, appears not to notice.

I have been standing in the line, and now it is my turn to order. I examine the selections on the gold-colored shelves in front of me. An attractive Salade Niçoise is tempting, with its dark greens and herbs and dewy crab meat. But just inches away, on a bed of ice, sit several brioches—croissants filled with various meats, vegetables, and cheeses. One made of spinach and parmesan sounds healthy, but I choose a more traditional one filled with freshly cut turkey and shredded Swiss cheese. A young woman lifts the brioche from the cooler and places it in a microwave oven. She looks Indian, and her manner is demure. She smiles from behind gold-rimmed glasses, revealing shiny white teeth. When I ask her to recommend a pastry, she suggests a pain au chocolat or a Napoléan, the thin-layered torte that the d'Or calls its specialty. As she describes the choices, my eyes fix on a tarte aux framboises, a fresh pastry shell laced with raspberry filling. It looks less fattening, and I decide to try it.

I watch as she pours the coffee from a silver urn and spins the milk in a heavy container for my café au lait. Her hand moves with care as the spindle whips the milk into a froth. I set the coffee, brioche, and pastry on a brown plastic tray and walk slowly through a door to an adjoining patio.

Crossing a slate floor, I select a table in the patio's corner. The sun filtering through the open slats of the roof has created warmth there. I sit looking out toward the interior of the café, as water gently trickles from a fountain a few feet away. Red geraniums, with buds in bloom, surround the pool. As I eat slowly, a cloud passes overhead, covering the sun for a moment but not lowering the temperature on this warm afternoon.

From outdoors, the interior of the Croissant d'Or looks different. The customers making their way through the line are now heading into the shadow that has engulfed the shop. Across the fountain, I see the Greek leaving with his sons. The brown-haired man has put the Sunday paper down and made his way over to the table of the younger man. He stands with his hand in his pocket, chatting easily as though with an old friend.

■ **Reflecting on Style**

The essay is understated, emphasizing unusual or unexpected discoveries about Le Croissant d'Or's patrons and ambiance. Given the focus on uncovering or unearthing unusual details, it is appropriate to find a blend of periodic and cumulative, or loose, sentences. By opening the essay with a periodic sentence, "When you walk through the doors of Le Croissant d'Or Patisserie in the French Quarter of New Orleans, you feel you've stepped into a café off the Champs-Élysées," I hold readers in suspense as they await my comparison of Le Croissant d'Or to a famous street in Paris, underscoring its authentic French decor and the sense of being transported to another country.

The same emphasis on surprising insights also makes the essay's frequent use of cumulative sentences appropriate since free modifiers allow me to add details to the main clause as fresh discoveries come to light. Here is an example: "The dim winter sun filters through clear glass windows on a Sunday afternoon, dividing the room in half, part in the shadows." I could have stopped after the main, or base, clause about the sun filtering through windows, but adding details about light severing the room and creating shadows reveals a new perspective on the d'Or, the sense of something riven, perhaps echoing an internal split or conflict.

Other parts of the essay also feature the idea of antithesis or opposition, with contrasts such as light and darkness, young and old, inside and outside dominating the writing. Given these opposing elements, the scheme of parenthesis, or interruption, seems apt, as it does in the sentence, "Red geraniums, with buds in bloom, surround the pool." The interruption, almost like an aside, or perhaps an arbiter, focuses on geranium buds in bloom, calling attention to living elements rather than dead or decaying ones.

In light of the somewhat tentative nature of the piece, it is not surprising that parenthesis—interruption—occasionally overlaps with apposition, the addition of an explanatory fact or detail, as it does in the following sentence: "Sixteen round tables, *all white*, are positioned casually around the restaurant, surrounded by chairs with wire backs that curve up into a heart shape." The case for "all white" as apposition, adding details about table color, is that the sentence simply makes an observation; however, a case can also be made for parenthesis, the interruption indicating an emphasis on interior uniformity that exists despite the essay's overall focus on subverting normal expectations.

An even stronger case for parenthesis, as opposed to apposition, can be made in the sentence, "The young man, a red scarf around his neck, appears not to notice." Here, interrupting the normal flow of the sentence seems likely in that the clause "a red scarf around his neck" calls attention to a dichotomy in the essay between introversion and extroversion. With the protectiveness of a scarf covering the young man up, in addition to his silence, introversion seems to win out, and he "appears not to notice" the other man.

The argument for parenthesis also seems persuasive since it focuses on the color red, which resonates in many ways throughout the essay, from the explicit mention of red geraniums and a (red) raspberry filling to the implicit mention of chairs with wire backs that "curve up into a heart shape" and the pervasive warm sun in the afternoon. The bold "red" perhaps goes along with a sense of wonder and openness in the essay, seen in the use of polysyndeton, an abundance of conjunctions, reflected in my use of "and":

> An attractive Salade Niçoise is tempting, with its dark greens *and* herbs *and* dewy crab meat.

Polysyndeton emphasizes the way the salade niçoise appeals, the use of "and" giving each new ingredient fresh life, as the whole of the salad ends up being more than the sum of its individual parts.

■ Revising with Style

Since my interest in the essay seems to be to question, or disrupt, our traditional ways of thinking about a café visit, I could do more to capture the essence of Le Croissant d'Or. In light of my emphasis on foreignness—in the international "feel" of the café and in my own observations—the use of anastrophe, or inverted word order, along with asyndeton, the absence of conjunctions, would help show how a sense of solitude seems to build in intensity and pace. Thus, after writing about going "through a door to an adjoining patio," I might add the following:

> As a light breeze blows, I notice the solitude of the outdoor space, its trees barren, tables empty, pigeons absent, departed, perhaps, for a more inhabited locale.

In this sentence, anastrophe provides syntax similar to French, in which adjectives follow the nouns they modify: "trees barren, tables empty, pigeons absent." The scheme puts emphasis on the adjectives "barren," "empty," and "absent," connected to solitude, a focus throughout the essay. Asyndeton, the omission of conjunctions, quickens the pace; by leaving out the *and* that would normally proceed "pigeons," the deserted nature of the location is intensified.

After using asyndeton, I add a free modifier: "departed, perhaps, for a more inhabited location." The word "departed" builds on "absent," and the free modifier contrasts the empty patio with "a more inhabited locale." At the same time, it uses a hedge, "perhaps," adding to the overall tentativeness or uncertainty of the essay.

While the essay hints at an affinity for nature, focusing on sunlight, the outdoors, geraniums, and a fountain, the allusions sometimes seem too understated, diminishing the overall effect. That omission might be remedied by turning to one of the restorative natural images in the essay: water. One option is to revise the sentence about water trickling from a fountain, and to add other sentences, all ending with *water*, using the scheme of epistrophe, the repetition of the same word at the end of successive clauses.

> I sit looking toward the interior of the café, the fountain's gentle trickle, just feet away, drawing my eyes toward the water. Peace, tranquility, reflection seem to flow from the same source: the fountain's water. Muted voices inside, silent spaces outside, all seem joined by one common theme: the sound of water.

The advantage of epistrophe in this case is to join together some of the oppositions—interior and exterior, silence and sound, crowded and solo spaces. By focusing on water, I am able to show more of a union between the essay narrator as observer of the scene around them and the narrator as active participant, drawing peace, tranquility, and reflection from the sound of water. The revised paragraph results from my deliberate, and artistic, use of style.

References

Abbey, Edward. 1968. *Desert Solitaire: A Season in the Wilderness.* New York: Simon & Schuster.

Allison, Dorothy. 1995. "From *Two or Three Things I Know for Sure.*" In *Available Means: An Anthology of Women's Rhetoric(s)*, edited by Joy Ritchie and Kate Ronald, 436–53. Pittsburgh, PA: University of Pittsburgh Press.

Angelou, Maya. 1969. *I Know Why the Caged Bird Sings.* New York: Random House.

Anzaldúa, Gloria. 1987. *Borderlands/La Frontera: The New Mestiza.* 4th ed. San Francisco, CA: Aunt Lute.

Aristotle. 2007. *On Rhetoric: A Theory of Civic Discourse.* 2nd ed. Translated by George A. Kennedy. New York: Oxford University Press.

Augustine. 1991. *The Confessions of Saint Augustine.* Translated by Henry Chadwick. New York: Oxford University Press.

Bartholomae, David. 1986. "Inventing the University." *Journal of Basic Writing* 5 (1): 4–23.

Bateman, Donald R., and Frank J. Zidonis. 1964. *The Effect of Knowledge of Generative Grammar upon the Growth of Language Complexity.* Columbus: The Ohio State University Press.

Bawarshi, Anis S., and Mary Jo Reiff. 2010. *Genre: An Introduction to History, Theory, Research, and Pedagogy.* Reference Guides to Rhetoric and Composition. West Lafayette, IN: Parlor.

DOI: 10.7330/9781607328100.c013

Berra, Yogi. 2010. *The Yogi Book*. New York: Workman.

Bloom, Amy. 2002. "The Body Lies: Female-to-Male Transsexuals." In *Normal: Transsexual CEOs, Crossdressing Cops, and Hermaphrodites with Attitude*, 1–48. New York: Vintage Books.

Bloom, Harold. 1996. *Maya Angelou's I Know Why the Caged Bird Sings*. Broomall, PA: Chelsea House.

Boime, Albert. 1984. "Van Gogh's *Starry Night*: A History of Matter, and a Matter of History." *Arts Magazine* 59 (4): 92–95.

Borland, Hal. 1964. *Sundial of the Seasons: A Selection of Outdoor Editorials from The New York Times*. New York: J. B. Lippincott.

Brooks, David. 2001. "One Nation, Slightly Divisible." *Atlantic* (December): 53–65.

Brooks, Phyllis. 1973. "Mimesis: Grammar and the Echoing Voice." *College English* 35 (2): 161–68. https://doi.org/10.2307/375442.

Brown, Dee. 1975. *Bury My Heart at Wounded Knee: An Indian History of the American West*. New York: Random House.

Brueggemann, Brenda Jo. 1990. "Signs and Numbers of the Times: Harper's 'Index' as an Essay Prompt." *College Composition and Communication* 41 (2): 220–22.

Bruner, Jerome. 1996. *The Culture of Education*. Boston, MA: Harvard University Press.

Burke, Kenneth. 1931. *Counter-Statement*. Berkeley: University of California Press.

Canagarajah, Suresh. 2011. "Afterword: World Englishes as Code-Meshing." In *Code-Meshing as World English: Pedagogy, Policy, Performance*, edited by Vershawn Ashanti Young and Aja Y. Martinez, 273–81. Urbana, IL: NCTE.

Capote, Truman. 1965. *In Cold Blood*. New York: Vintage Books.

Carr, Nicolas. 2008. "Is Google Making Us Stupid?" *Atlantic* July/August. https://www.theatlantic.com/magazine/archive/2008/07/is-google-making-us-stupid/306868/.

Carson, Rachel. 1962. *Silent Spring*. New York: Houghton Mifflin.

Christensen, Francis. 1963. "A Generative Rhetoric of the Sentence." *College Composition and Communication* 14 (3): 155–61. https://doi.org/10.2307/355051.

Churchill, Winston. 1930. *My Early Life: A Roving Commission*. New York: Scribner's-Macmillan.

Cicero. 1939. *Orator*. Translated by H. M. Hubbell. Cambridge, MA: Harvard University Press. https://doi.org/10.4159/DLCL.marcus_tullius_cicero-orator.1939.

Clark, Herbert H., and Susan E. Haviland. 1977. "Comprehension and the Given-New Contract." In *Discourse Production and Comprehension*, edited by Roy O. Freedle, 1–40. Norwood, NJ: Ablex.

Coates, Ta-Nehisi. 2015. *Between the World and Me*. New York: Spiegel & Grau.

Corbett, Edward P. J., and Robert J. Connors. 1999. *Style and Statement*. New York: Oxford University Press.

Curzan, Anne. 2013. "Rhetoric: Positive, Negative, or Both?" *That's What They Say*. Michigan Radio. Ann Arbor, MI: WUOM, July 28. http://michiganradio.org/post/rhetoric-postive-negative-or-both.

D'Angelo, Frank. 1973. "Imitation and Style." *College Composition and Communication* 24 (3): 283–90. https://doi.org/10.2307/356855.

Damon, Matt. 2016. "Matt Damon's Commencement Address." *MIT News*, June 3. http://news.mit.edu/2016/matt-damon-commencement-address-0603.

Davis, Lennard J. 2001. "Visualizing the Disabled Body: The Classical Nude and the Fragmented Torso." In *The Norton Anthology of Theory and Criticism*, edited by Vincent B. Leitch and Jeffrey Williams, 2400–2421. New York: Norton.

de Certeau, Michel. 1984. *The Practice of Everyday Life*. Translated by Steven F. Rendall. Berkeley: University of California Press.

Delpit, Lisa. 1995. *Other People's Children: Cultural Conflict in the Classroom*. New York: W. W. Norton.

de Saussure, Ferdinand. 2011. *Course in General Linguistics*. Edited by Perry Meisel and Haun Saussy. Translated by Wade Baskin. New York: Columbia University Press.

Didion, Joan. 1961. "Goodbye to All That." In *Slouching Towards Bethlehem*, 225–38. New York: Farrar, Straus and Giroux.

Dillard, Annie. 1974. *Pilgrim at Tinker Creek*. New York: Harper's Magazine Press.

Dillard, Annie. 1995. "Seeing." In *The Art of the Personal Essay: An Anthology from the Classical Era to the Present*, edited by Phillip Lopate, 693–706. New York: Anchor Books.

Elbow, Peter. 2012. *Vernacular Eloquence: What Speech Can Bring to Writing*. New York: Oxford University Press. https://doi.org/10.1093/acprof:osobl/9780199782505.001.0001.

Erasmus, Desiderius. 1512. *De Copia*. Paris: Josse Bade.

Fahnestock, Jeanne. 1999. *Rhetorical Figures in Science*. New York: Oxford University Press.

Farquhar, Michael. 2015. *Bad Days in History: A Gleefully Grim Chronicle of Misfortune, Mayhem, and Misery for Every Day of the Year*. New York: National Geographic.

FitzGerald, William. 2013. "Stylistic Sandcastles: Rhetorical Figures as Composition's Bucket and Spade." In *The Centrality of Style*, edited by Mike Duncan and Star Medzerian Vanguri, 37–56. Fort Collins, CO: Parlor.

Flower, Linda. 1979. "Writer-Based Prose: A Cognitive Basis for Problems in Writing." *College English* 41 (1): 19–37. https://doi.org /10.2307/376357.

Foucault, Michel. 1970. *The Order of Things: An Archaeology of the Human Sciences*. New York: Vintage Books.

Garber, Megan. 2013. "English Has a New Preposition, Because Internet." *Atlantic*, November 9. https://www.theatlantic.com /technology/archive/2013/11/english-has-a-new-preposition -because-internet/281601/.

Garza, Edward Santos. 2012. "Playing the Whole Court: A Stylistic Analysis of David Foster Wallace's 'Derivative Sport in Tornado Alley.'" Unpublished manuscript.

Gilyard, Keith. 1991. *Voices of the Self: A Study of Language Competence*. Detroit, MI: Wayne State University Press.

Gopnik, Adam. 2017. "Hemingway as Sensualist." *New Yorker*, July 3. https://www.newyorker.com/magazine/2017/07/03/hemingway -the-sensualist.

Hawking, Stephen. 1988. *A Brief History of Time*. New York: Bantam Books.

Herr, Michael. 1977. *Dispatches*. New York: Knopf.

Hess, Amanda. 2015. "When You 'Literally Can't Even' Understand Your Teenager." *New York Times Magazine*, June 9. https://www .nytimes.com/2015/06/14/magazine/when-you-literally-cant -even-understand-your-teenager.html.

Holleran, Andrew. 1988. "Ground Zero." In *Ground Zero*, by Andrew Holleran, 19–28. New York: Morrow.

Halloran, S. Michael, and Merrill D. Whitburn. 1982. "Ciceronian Rhetoric and the Rise of Science: The Plain Style Reconsidered." *The Rhetorical Tradition and Modern Writing*. Edited by James J. Murphy, 58–72. New York: MLA.

Hunt, Kellogg W. 1965. *Grammatical Structures Written at Three Grade Levels*. Champaign, IL: NCTE.

Junod, Tom. 2003. "The Falling Man." *Esquire*, September 9. https:// www.esquire.com/news-politics/a48031/the-falling-man-tom -junod/.

Kafka, Franz. 2016. *The Metamorphosis*. Norton Critical ed. Edited by Mark M. Anderson. Translated by Susan Bernofsky. New York: W. W. Norton.

Kamiya, Gary. 1996. "Transgressing the Transgressors: Toward a Transformative Hermeneutics of Total Bullshit." *Salon* 17 May. http://www.salon.com/media/media960517.html.

Kempton, Murray. 1955. *Part of Our Time: Some Ruins and Monuments of the Thirties*. New York: New York Review Books.

Kennedy, John F. 1961. "First Inaugural Address." January 20. https://www.jfklibrary.org/Asset-Viewer/BqXIEM9F4024ntF17 SVA/A.aspx.

Kent, Thomas, ed. 1999. *Post-Process Theory: Beyond the Writing-Process Paradigm*. Carbondale: Southern Illinois University Press.

King, Martin Luther, Jr. 1963. "I Have a Dream." American History from Revolution to Reconstruction. documents/1951-/martin -luther-kings-i-have-a-dream-speech-august-28–1963.php.

Knibb, Kate. 2014. "Stealing My Brother's Walkman." Gizmodo. gizmodo.com.au/2014/07/stealing-my-brothers-walkman/.

Krakauer, Jon. 1996. *Into the Wild*. New York: Anchor Books.

Lanham, Richard A. 1983a. *Analyzing Prose*. 2nd ed. London: Continuum.

Lanham, Richard A. 1983b. *Literacy and the Survival of Humanism*. New Haven, CT: Yale University Press.

Lanham, Richard A. 1991. *A Handlist of Rhetorical Terms*. 2nd ed. Berkeley: University of California Press.

Lanham, Richard A. 2006. *The Economics of Attention: Style and Substance in the Age of Information*. Chicago, IL: University of Chicago Press.

Lanham, Richard A. 2007. *Revising Prose*. 5th ed. New York: Pearson/ Longman.

Levine, Steven Z. 1996. "Manet's Man Meets the Gleam of Her Gaze: A Psychoanalytic Novel." In *Twelve Views of Manet's* Bar, edited by Bradford R. Collins, 250–77. Princeton, NJ: Princeton University Press.

Lincoln, Abraham. 1863. "The Gettysburg Address." Abraham Lincoln Online. http://www.abrahamlincolnonline.org/lincoln/speeches /gettysburg.htm.

Lindbergh, Anne Morrow. 1955. *Gift from the Sea*. New York: Pantheon.

Luke, Timothy W. 1997. "Museum Pieces: Politics and Knowledge at the American Museum of Natural History." *Australasian Journal of American Studies* 16 (2): 1–28.

Lupton, Mary Jane. 1998. *Maya Angelou: A Critical Companion*. Greenwood, CT: Greenwood.

Macaulay, Rose. 1966. *Pleasure of Ruins*. London: Thames and Hudson.

Marche, Stephen. 2012. "Is Facebook Making Us Lonely?" *Atlantic* (May 15): 60–69.

Márquez, Gabriel García. 1997. *News of a Kidnapping*. Translated by Edith Grossman. New York: Vintage International.

McPhee, John. 1976. "The Search for Marvin Gardens." In *The John McPhee Reader*, edited by William L. Howarth, 309–21. New York: Farrar, Straus, and Giroux.

Milic, Louis T. 1966. "Metaphysics in the Criticism of Style." *College Composition and Communication* 17 (3): 124–29. https://doi.org /10.2307/354426.

Miller, Carolyn. 1984. "Genre as Social Action." *Quarterly Journal of Speech* 70 (2): 151–67. https://doi.org/10.1080/0033563840938 3686.

Momaday, N. Scott. 1976. *The Way to Rainy Mountain*. Albuquerque: University of New Mexico Press.

Monette, Paul. 1992. *Becoming a Man: Half a Life Story*. San Francisco, CA: HarperCollins.

Mukherjee, Siddhartha. 2010. *The Emperor of All Maladies: A Biography of Cancer*. New York: Scribner.

Murphy, James J. 1987. *Quintilian: On the Teaching of Speaking and Writing. Translations from Books One, Two, and Ten of the Institutio oratoria*. Carbondale: Southern Illinois University Press.

Murry, John Middleton. 1922. *The Problem of Style*. New York: Oxford University Press.

National Council of Teachers of English. 2016. "The Doublespeak Award." http://www.ncte.org/volunteer/groups/publiclangcom /doublespeakaward.

New York Times. 1981. "The Private Hemingway." *The New York Times Magazine*, February 15, 1981.

Obama, Barack. 1995. *Dreams from My Father: A Story of Race and Inheritance*. New York: Three Rivers-Crown.

Obama, Barack. 2009. "First Inaugural Address." Bartleby.com.
http://www.bartleby.com/124/pres68.html.

Obama, Barack. 2016. "Remarks by the President at Commencement
Address at Rutgers, the State University of New Jersey." The White
House. President Barack Obama. https://obamawhitehouse
.archives.gov/the-press-office/2016/05/15/remarks-president
-commencement-address-rutgers-state-university-new.

O'Hare, Frank. 1973. *Sentence Combining: Improving Student Writing
without Formal Grammar Instruction.* Champaign, IL: NCTE.

O'Hare, Frank. 1985. *Sentencecraft: A Course in Sentence-Combining.*
New York: Silver Burdett Ginn Religion.

Ohmann, Richard. 1967. "Prolegomena to the Analysis of Prose Style."
In *Essays on the Language of Literature,* edited by Seymour Chat-
man and Samuel R Levin, 410. New York: Houghton, Mifflin.

Orenstein, Peggy. 2010. "I Tweet, Therefore I Am." *New York Times
Magazine,* July 30. http://www.nytimes.com/2010/08/01
/magazine/01wwln-lede-t.html.

Orwell, George. 1968. "The Politics of the English Language." In Vol. 4
of *The Collected Essays, Journalism and Letters of George Orwell.*
1st ed. Edited by Sonia Orwell and Ian Angos, 127–40. Harcourt
Brace Jovanovich.

Paine, Thomas. 1776. *The Crisis.* UShistory.org. http://www.ushistory
.org/Paine/crisis/index.htm.

Quintilian. 1921. *Institutio Oratoria.* 4 vols. Translated by Harold
Edgeworth Butler. Cambridge, MA: Harvard University Press.

Rodriguez, Richard. 1992. *Days of Obligation: An Argument with My
Mexican Father.* New York: Penguin.

Rodriguez, Richard. 1995. "Late Victorians." In *The Art of the Personal
Essay: An Anthology from the Classical Era to the Present,* edited
by Phillip Lopate, 756–90. New York: Anchor Books.

Ross, Alex. 2007. *The Rest Is Noise: Listening to the Twentieth Century.*
New York: Picador.

Sanders, Scott Russell. 1995. "Under the Influence." In *The Art of the
Personal Essay: An Anthology from the Classical Era to the Present,*
edited by Phillip Lopate, 733–44. New York: Anchor Books.

Smitherman, Geneva. 1977. *Talkin and Testifyin: The Language of
Black America.* Detroit, MI: Wayne State University Press.

Sontag, Susan. 1977. *Illness as Metaphor and AIDS and Its Metaphors.*
New York: Picador.

Spencer, Charles. 1997. "Full Text of Earl Spencer's Funeral Oration." BBC.com. http://www.bbc.co.uk/news/special/politics97/diana /spencerfull.html.

Stein, Gertrude. 1933. *The Autobiography of Alice B. Toklas*. New York: Vintage Books.

Strong, William. 1994. *Sentence-Combining: A Composing Book*. New York: McGraw-Hill.

Strunk, William Jr., and E. B. White. 2000 (1979). *The Elements of Style*. 4th ed. New York: Longman.

Taylor, Rich. 1978. *Modern Classics: The Great Cars of the Postwar Era*. New York: Charles Scribner's Sons.

Thompson, Hunter S. 1973. *Fear and Loathing on the Campaign Trail '72*. New York: Simon & Schuster.

Thoreau, Henry David. 2016. *Walden*. New York: Tarcher/Perigee-Penguin Random House.

Trilling, Lionel. 1950. *The Liberal Imagination: Essays on Literature and Society*. New York: Viking.

Tuchman, Barbara. 1962. *The Guns of August*. New York: Scribner.

Tufte, Virginia. 1971. *Grammar as Style*. New York: Holt, Rinehart and Winston.

Turkle, Sherry. 2012. *Alone Together: Why We Expect More from Technology and Less from Each Other*. New York: Basis Books.

Twain, Mark. 1994. *Adventures of Huckleberry Finn*. Mineola, NY: Dover.

Twain, Mark. 1996. *The Innocents Abroad*. New York: Oxford University Press.

van Gogh, Vincent. 1889. *Starry Night*. Oil on Canvas. New York, Museum of Modern Art.

Vance, J. D. 2016. *Hillbilly Elegy: A Memoir of a Family and a Culture in Crisis*. New York: Harper Collins.

Wallace, David Foster. 1997. *A Supposedly Fun Thing I'll Never Do Again*. New York: Little, Brown.

White, E. B. 1995. "Once More to the Lake." In *The Art of the Personal Essay: An Anthology from the Classical Era to the Present*, edited by Phillip Lopate, 533–38. New York: Anchor Books.

Wilford, John Noble. 1969. "A Powdery Surface Is Closely Explored." *New York Times*, June 21.

Wilson, Rob. 1994. "Cyborg America: Policing the Social Sublime in 'Robocop' and 'Robocop 2.'" In *The Administration of Aesthetics:*

Censorship, Political Criticism, and the Public Sphere, edited by Richard Burt, 289–306. Minneapolis: University of Minnesota Press.

Winchester, Otis, ed. 1972. *The Sound of Your Voice: Readings for Writers.* Boston, MA: Allyn and Bacon.

Young, Vershawn Ashanti. 2010. "Should Writers Use They Own English?" *Iowa Journal of Cultural Studies* 12 (1): 110–17. http://digital.lib.uiowa.edu/ijcs/ijcs1213-10.htm.

Young, Vershawn Ashanti. 2014. "Introduction: Are You a Part of the Conversation?" In *Other People's English: Code-Meshing, Code-Switching, and African American Literacy,* edited by Vershawn Ashanti Young, Rusty Barrett, Y'Shawnda Young-Rivera, and Kim Brian Lovejoy, 1–11. New York: Teachers College Press.

Young, Vershawn Ashanti, and Aja Y. Martinez. 2011. *Code-Meshing as World English.* Urbana, IL: NCTE.

Zinsser, William. 1980. *On Writing Well: An Informal Guide to Writing Nonfiction.* 2nd ed. New York: Harper and Row.

Illustration Credits

Starry Night (*La nuit etoilée*) by Vincent van Gogh, painting, oil on canvas, Saint-Rémy, June 1889 (MOMA)
CREDIT: Acquired through the Lillie P. Bliss Bequest, Digital Image © The Museum of Modern Art/Licensed by SCALA/Art Resource, NY

Abraham Lincoln and the Gettysburg Address
CREDIT: Used with the permission of www.lapopart.com

"Think outside the box" visual representation
CREDIT: "Think outside the Box" artwork by Zero Dean

From Thomas Paine's *The Crisis*
CREDIT: Used with the permission of Jesus Perez

Classification system from Foucault's *The Order of Things*
CREDIT: Used with the permission of Jesus Perez

Edited version of the Declaration of Independence
CREDIT: Thomas Jefferson's Draft of the Declaration of Independence, June–July 1776, from Library of Congress, The Thomas Jefferson Papers

Representation of David Brooks's sentence using generative rhetoric
CREDIT: Used with the permission of Jesus Perez

Illustration of widespread use of Twitter and Hashtags in writing
CREDIT: Used with the permission of Zaheer Mohiuddin

Variation on Standard Edited English
CREDIT: Used with the permission of Shutterstock

Sign representing the intersection of cohesion and coherence
CREDIT: Used with the permission of Getty Images (US), Inc./iStock

Representation of style using an allusion to "Got Milk?" campaign
CREDIT: Used with the permission of Shutterstock

Le Croissant d'Or Patisserie in New Orleans
CREDIT: Used with the permission of Rebecca Todd

About the Author

PAUL BUTLER is associate professor in the Department of English at the University of Houston and is recognized as an expert on the study of style in rhetoric and composition. He is the author of *The Writer's Style*, *Out of Style*, and *Style in Rhetoric and Composition*. His recent scholarship focuses on the intersection of style, the public sphere, multimodal composition, and the digital humanities.

Index

INDEX